FROM QUIET MOMENTS

FROM QUIET MOMENTS

SPIRITUAL AWAKENING

BOOK I

PATRICK A. SCHIAVONE

ISBNs:

Paperback: 979-8-9910671-7-1

eBook: 979-8-9910671-4-0

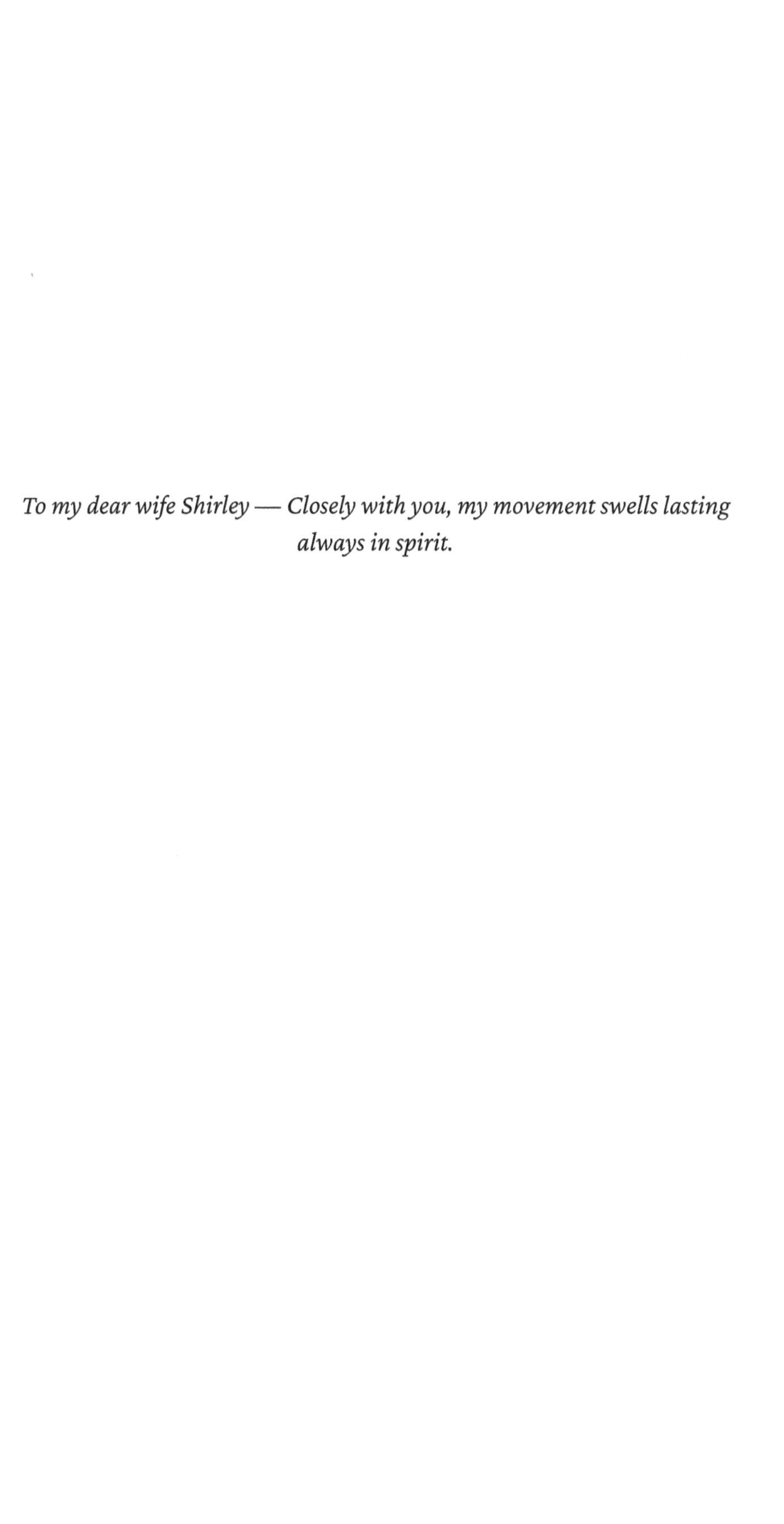

To my dear wife Shirley — Closely with you, my movement swells lasting always in spirit.

"We are loved and cherished. That is all we need to know."

— CHANNELED WRITING

CONTENTS

INTRODUCTION

Take a moment, if you will, to imagine the face of a newborn baby (perhaps your own child or one you love). What do you notice is happening for that baby? What do you notice happening in you as you behold this new Being who has just entered the world? We may feel a state of awe at their beingness, as we see how they hold the essence of who they are without any struggle or strain. Babies remind us that our rightful state of existence is grace, holiness and joy.

As we grow up and learn the ways of the world, we lose our innocence, and often our joy and happiness, too. Spirituality, and the spiritual path, is how we make our way back to knowing and being who we really are. As we allow ourselves to be immersed in the spiritual realm, we find the joy and freedom we once experienced as a baby. We see through a clear lens who we really are and who we have always been. The spiritual world beckons us to come Home, to return to its garden of purity, holiness and joy.

The spiritual seeker dedicates themselves to a path that leads them back to their True Self. As they walk this path, although seemingly alone, they walk it with the full support and love of God, who holds them as a loving parent would their child in every step they take. This book, and the trilogy of which it is a part, is designed to serve as a companion for spiritual seekers along their path back Home.

Life is our training ground, challenging us to see our spiritual nature and origins, to look at ourselves fresh and realize the innocence and joy of who we really are. We learn in our own way and yet we all walk together with the same goal: to spiritually awaken to the vast and infinite realm of Spirit. This awakening brings us comfort, direction and fulfillment with the recognition and remembrance of our true existence. This path helps us mature into powerful beings, into our True Self nature, which does not know doubt or fear but only the existence of truth.

We don't develop our spirituality simply to live the kind of life we want to live. We develop our spirituality to realize who we really are. For, it is from this awareness that we truly express the Father. We allow Spirit to express itself through our unique prism of talents and abilities. We therefore allow co-creation to occur. Spirit is the force and we are the vehicle for its manifestation in the physical world. We enter into true service to our inner Self and to our brothers and sisters, i.e. humanity. We are simply expressions of all that is, nothing more and nothing less. *How could it be any other way?* Our voice must be heard and our actions must be seen in order to affect a better world; not for our sake, but to bring our Father's gifts into it. These gifts are not only our heritage, but the heritage of all.

Once we seekers experience such an awakening, we become more available for a true and meaningful life of service to others. In service, we can take the spiritual insights and knowings we receive and put them into aligned action in our lives. We stand with God the Father and all our brothers and sisters in union and purpose as we bring true meaning into our lives. We are and express love, unencumbered and free flowing, because it is who we are and who we are meant to be. We share the gift of our unique abilities and talents with others so they can remember and benefit from their spiritual heritage. We walk together on the road Home to freedom, in innocence and joy: our birthrights.

The *From Quiet Moments* Trilogy, which you hold in your hands now, is a companion and guidebook to support and enhance your spiritual journey. It offers channeled messages brought straight from the Spiritual Realms to our Earthly Realm in an accessible way, to bring you solace, encouragement, remembrance, and joy along your own unique path home to your True Self. These books and their messages are designed to meet you wherever you find yourself on the path, and to walk with you forward into the life that is meant for you.

The intrinsic value of the *From Quiet Moments* Trilogy lies in its teachings on the *descension* into the truth rather than the *ascension* to it. This means we don't have to go "up and out" of our lives to receive truth, but rather, we drop more deeply "down and into" our lives. This path of descension changes not only thinking but consciousness. While the messages of this trilogy are aligned with ancient wisdom, this body of work transcends the esoteric and mysterious by conveying true spiritual principles in a simple and understandable way, allowing for its easy integration into every day life.

From Quiet Moments provides the following unique benefits to you, the reader:

- The Trilogy provides an opportunity for you as a spiritual seeker to partake in its writing regardless of wherever you are on your spiritual path.
- Through its question-and-answer format, it provides simple and clear messages that are easy to contemplate and assimilate into your lived reality.
- The Trilogy uniquely delivers spiritual knowledge and steady encouragement to trust your inner voice as you readily integrate the wisdom, and your experience of it, into your everyday life.

- Its messages incorporate easily into any existing individual spiritual practice.
- It provides a spiritual roadmap for how to move through the different phases of your spiritual journey and provides the principles necessary to advance your spiritual growth.
- Finally, it provides a consistent pathway of clarity, trust and inspiration to motivate you, the spiritual seeker, to create the spiritual growth and fulfillment you are seeking.

Although the Trilogy books were written in a sequential order, which reflects my own spiritual journey, they do not necessarily need to be read sequentially. Each book stands on its own, providing the reader the choice to partake from where they are so inclined. This furthers the intention behind this work to be non-prescriptive. I encourage you to find your way through the Trilogy using the guidance of your own intuition, your own inner voice. I have made my share of mistakes in my life by listening to my head instead of my intuition and heart. As I continue to walk on my spiritual journey, I have learned to trust more and more in myself and in the guidance that sets my life's direction. I hope you'll give this a try here as well.

To help you decide where to begin, I have listed each book's theme followed by a more descriptive explanation. Book I focuses on Spiritual Awakening, Book II centers on Spiritual Searching, and Book III's theme is Spiritual Action. At the end of each description, I'll offer a profile of the respective spiritual seeker for whom each book most closely corresponds.

The *From Quiet Moments* Trilogy progressively takes the seeker from the discovery of their spiritual nature, through their search in affirming their True Self, and finally into asserting their essence through action into the physical world. It assists the spiritual seeker in their spiritual practice, which is the foundation of spiritual growth.

BOOK I: SPIRITUAL AWAKENING IS ABOUT DISCOVERY

Book I's theme is Spiritual Awakening, which is about discovering there is more than meets the eye – that is, more than just the physical. This denotes the beginning stages of the spiritual journey. The tone of Book I is *invitational* in that we are invited to partake in our personal journey of realizing we are a spiritual being who has taken on a body to live in the physical world.

While this book will support any spiritual seeker, it is intended for the *Uncertain Spiritual Seeker,* who is walking away from the restraints put upon them all their life. They no longer find the answers they need from their religious beliefs. They look to better their health, relieve stress and find emotional support. Some might be acting in a rebellious way toward the church and others are simply looking for more and deeper spiritual experiences, which are personalized and meaningful for them. They are uncertain because they have become more disillusioned with their current beliefs and now seek alternative spiritual knowledge. They keep moving forward in the promise that their spiritual journey will give them the peace and happiness they are seeking.

BOOK II: SPIRITUAL SEARCHING IS ABOUT EXPLORATION OF TRUE SELF

Book II's theme of Spiritual searching is about the exploration of True Self. In our spiritual searching, we experience a decomposition or dissolution of our old beliefs. Through this dismantling, a new foundation is formed, which leads to a firmness of thought, a developing trust, and eventually a permanent *knowing* of our True Self. Established in this state of True Self consciousness, we can see and realize our spiritual nature while going about our daily lives. The tone of this book is *affirmational,* as we continually affirm who we really are.

While this book will support all seekers, its primary intended reader is the *Emerging Spiritual Seeker,* who is pursuing their spiritual path and still working to find peace inside themselves. Like a perpetual explorer, they move from one spiritual practice and belief to another, some out of intellectual curiosity, and others with a genuine intention to delve deeper into their inner soul and live life with greater purpose. For some, this may lead to new belief systems and alternative spiritual communities, while others may return full circle to their original religion with a better understanding and appreciation of it.

BOOK III: SPIRITUAL ACTION IS ABOUT ACTING FROM YOUR TRUE SELF

Book III's theme of Spiritual Action is where we are awakened, know our True Self and are now equipped to move through and overcome the obstacles the physical world puts before us. It reveals to us that, as a spiritual being in a physical world, we have no limitations. Thus, we can move through any ego thinking and drop the appearance of any restrictions that seemingly hold us from expressing our True Self. This expression brings us fulfillment and subsequently joy. The tone of Book III is *authoritative,* since it is in direct conversation with the God, Himself.

While this book will support any seeker, it is intended most for the *Devoted Spiritual Seeker,* who has broken free of the confines of past beliefs and created their own spiritual philosophy. They follow their inner voice using their talents and abilities while expressing their true nature. Their life has meaning. They envision a fulfilling life as realizing their union with life itself. They are devoted and willing to be who they really are and to "push forward" the good within themselves out into the world.

Please note that all three books of the Trilogy are channeled. However, the orientation of Books I and II are geared toward humanity, the "We," with the intent of showing us that we are "all in this together" as we awaken to and remember our True Selves. Book III's orientation is towards the individual, the "You," who has come to Spiritual realization and created a devoted spiritual life. The individual is now provided the means to bring forth Spirit into the world through their actions, to affect the world in an altruistic and uplifting way.

MESSAGE TO THE SPIRITUAL SEEKER ABOUT BOOK I

Since we are here in Book I together now, let's dive a bit deeper into what you will find in this component of the Trilogy. Book I's theme is Spiritual Awakening. If you have recently started on your spiritual journey or if you have an inkling to do so, the words throughout these pages offer you the guidance and answers you are looking for. Whether you have been prompted by a traumatic event in your life, or you are leading a successful material life but are looking for a deeper meaning and purpose, this book is for you.

Keep in mind that you have drawn to yourself the knowledge that lies in these pages at a deeper level. Allow these words to speak the truth to you. As you will recognize early on, a specific question will not give you a specific answer; but instead will expose you to universal truth, which has no confines or limitation. However, as you spend time reading these words and allowing them to enter into your consciousness, they will guide you into the deeper meaning of your life.

True intent to grow in this knowledge is reflected by your willingness to set aside the time to read these words, allowing your mind to enter a restful state. Regardless of how and when you create a quiet time and space for yourself, remember that the words in these pages are meant specifically for your spiritual growth and to awaken you to who you really are.

At this point in your life, being attracted to this writing, you likely feel a need for Spiritual Awakening. Maybe you feel a slight impulse. Maybe a yearning or even an aching inside of you to awaken to a spiritual life. It does not matter, for now you are on the threshold of a true and powerful spiritual journey.

To achieve Self Awakening, there are twelve attributes or qualities that must be uncovered, developed and utilized. These twelve qualities are part of your spiritual "tool belt" that are instrumental to awaken you to a higher state of consciousness and serve you on the pathway to your True Self on this your Spiritual Awakening journey. The most prominent are Intention, Faith and Healing, and each of these is associated with another three qualities, described below in these sets of four. View these initial attributes not in a hard, fast or hierarchical way; but rather as a basis to the attributes associated with them that form the make up of who you really are.

Intention relates to Openness, Willingness and Courage

Intention is sparked by a need or desire for a change in your life. You intend to move forward in a certain direction in your life. While you might not be sure at this point what it is, you do know it has been stirred up from inside of you. Intention leads to *Openness,* which is the first step of your Spiritual Awakening. While you may not be sure of what to do or how to proceed, you are open to the possibilities that present themselves to you. Openness gives way to *Willingness.* For you are willing to put yourself forward, to do the work involved and to take the necessary steps. It is necessary to be willing; yet what actually sustains you is *Courage* because no matter how new or foreign this journey may seem, it is your Courage that you carry with you in every step that sustains you.

Faith calls for Trust, Diligence, and Steadfastness

Faith is very instrumental because it lights the way. It aids you in finding the right path for you to take. Faith is developed through *Trust* – trust in yourself and trust in the higher power that lives within you. Now that you know where you are going and you've built some Trust, you engage *Diligence*. Through Diligence, you apply yourself in a very conscientious way to the task at hand. It is through your Diligence that you start to realize results in your Spiritual Awakening process. Lastly, *Steadfastness* must be applied to your spiritual work. There may be pitfalls. There may be distractions. There may be a sense of weariness and a temptation to just give up. Yet, your Steadfastness will keep you going and bring you untold rewards on your Spiritual Awakening journey.

Healing requires Humility, Denunciation and Forgiveness

Through your Intention and Faith, *Healing* begins to occur in your life. The traumas, mistakes and regrets from the past surface in your consciousness with a clearer perspective so that you may now see them for what they truly are. This takes *Humility*, for through Humility you see your human imperfections. Once these imperfections are accepted, you are then able to *Denounce* any habits or behaviors you adopted because of them as you move forward on your spiritual path. These imperfections teach you to love yourself just the way that you are. By recognizing and accepting them, you set yourself free. Further, you Denounce that which no longer holds value for you and you stop making the same mistakes over and over again. Lastly and so importantly, you use *Forgiveness* to release yourself from all of the traumas, bad behavior and regrets from the past. You forgive yourself and you forgive those who trespassed against you. You literally heal yourself so that you can now wake up to your True Self.

In summary, it is through your *Intent* that you open yourself up to a successful spiritual life. *Faith* brings you forward on this journey as you bring all of yourself to it. Finally, *Healing* frees you to experience Spiritual Awakening.

TRILOGY'S MAIN THEMES

Now that you have a better understanding of the Trilogy and Book I in particular, let's dive a bit deeper into the key principles of spirituality that serve us through and across all three books.

The foundational principles threaded through the entire Trilogy are Free Will, Spiritual Practice, Devotion and Spiritual Heritage. By using these principles they will show you *how* to move along your spiritual path as you awaken to your spiritual nature, remember your True Self, and act from your True Self. These principles are *essential* to your success in realizing your spiritual heritage of a meaningful and purposeful life.

Free Will: Our Father's Most Precious Gift

No dogma or doctrine can bring us the peace and happiness we seek within ourselves. For in the end, we all must choose for ourselves and not from whatever anyone else says or does. This is the precious gift of free will. In life, as guide posts are presented to us, others fade away. We are invited not to attach to them but to allow our growth in consciousness, as we move forward on our spiritual path, choice by choice, with more confidence and certainty. Our choices have led us up to this point and they will continue to lead us further. From this perspective, Spirit is realized.

As we all take our individual paths to eternal happiness, we meet each other in true harmony and love, as we all enter into the Kingdom of our Father, who is one in us as we are one in Him. Through His most precious gift of free will, He displays His profound and eternal love for us. Beneath the tragedies in our lives, we find our way Home; and, as we drop the trappings of fear and judgment, we fully exercise our freedom to continually grow in the awareness of our Father.

It is always our free will choice and personal spiritual work that moves us along to a perfect union with our Father. A true source of guidance will always present us with the direction we need to go. In that way, it allows us the opportunity to exercise our free will, which is the only way to truly join with the Father.

Spiritual Practice: the Foundation for Spiritual Growth

Spiritual practice is the way we increase our awareness and spirituality. Our spiritual practice is comprised of three pillars: meditation, prayer and guidance. As we meditate, our mind becomes unencumbered and clear. As we pray, our heart becomes soft and vulnerable. Lastly, guidance unifies the soul. Guidance is initiated by simply asking for it. In the asking, we engage in conversation with the Father. As we converse with the Father, our soul develops an intimacy and then union with Him. It is from this union that the guidance we are seeking truly comes to us and we know what to do.

When we practice meditation, prayer and guidance, the signposts simply show up. These can arrive in the form of a person, a book, an event, and so on. No matter the form, our growing awareness from such signposts allows answers to be revealed to us and the way is made clear for us to proceed, no matter how difficult it is or how fearful we may feel.

Since we all come from different backgrounds, cultures, and religions, we all have choice in how to conduct our spiritual practice. It is through this practice that union with our Father is realized and enjoyed. From our own awareness and uniqueness, we choose what suits us at any particular time and what we feel will give us the most benefit. Our sincerity in performing our spiritual practice is what brings us a rich and abundant life to enjoy.

In our practice of meditation, prayer and guidance we open ourselves up to our True Self. The Trilogy assists us in obtaining guidance from our Father, which establishes a union with Him and welcomes Him into our everyday life. *From Quiet Moments'* writings bring the third pillar of our spiritual practice, guidance, alive so that we can then partake more readily in our redemption. These writings serve as a bridge to further questions that we then begin to ask, so we can receive the answers we seek to live in truth, peace and happiness.

Devotion Ensures Spiritual Fulfillment

Free will directs our spiritual practice and devotion energizes it. Devotion is the fuel we use to carry us to Spiritual Fulfillment. From spiritual practice, insights occur that clear the way. This inspires us to create. By creating, we become co-creators with the Father. Through co-creation, we join with Him. By joining with the Father, we become one with Him.

Only we can walk the path of devotion in our spiritual practice, which is the only way to truth and happiness. Guides, in the form of spiritual teachers, books, ancient traditions, religions and artifacts, may point us along the way by bringing us signs of our Father and how we play our part with Him. However, let us not be misled and put our faith in these things themselves, but instead keep our faith and belief firm as we devote ourselves to our Almighty Father with a love that burns so hot it overshadows all else.

Our Heritage is a Purposeful and Happy Life

We access our true heritage through our willingness and devotion to eliminate struggle. By verifying the truth of our existence and therefore living according to our purpose, we institute a free and happy life. We must stand up in purity, see ourselves in the light of the Father, and be a witness to heaven descending upon earth. This is truly our heritage and purpose because this is who we really are. We are our Father's children and we bring forth that which we are into the world.

Are we not being asked to usher in heaven upon earth? Are we not loved deeply and eternally by our Father? Does He not ask us to join with Him in all that we do? Are we not Him as he holds us in His expression?

What must we believe in but Him and His holiness that lives within us? Let us not put anyone or anything before Him because we are Him and He is us. In His glory may we all live and express Him with humility and devotion in Holy Union.

As the flow of our Father's love flows through us, the realization of His power becomes evident. It is in this union that our hopes are met, and peace and happiness become apparent. Only through our willingness to put down the false gods of our pride, can Spirit enter into our lives and become a living Presence. We have entered into His Kingdom now and forever. We must always choose from our innate ability to accept and affirm our heritage: the Kingdom of God which lives within us.

MY OWN SPIRITUAL PATH

Below I briefly describe myself and how this writing came to be. Its emergence occurred only after many years in search of spiritual freedom. As with all of us, certain events set the direction for our lives. My father died suddenly when I was only six years old. A lurking, persistent feeling that "something is not right" was finally rectified decades later when I found out that my father took his own life. My father's absence left empty his role as a provider. This created an atmosphere of spartan living in our home, accompanied by austerity and restriction. My mother's character included a deep sense of responsibility and earnestness to care for her children. It was her tenacity and perseverance in the face of such an abrupt trauma that gave her the strength to see us through such adversity. For this I am forever thankful to my Mother and I love her always.

My Mother's zeal to be protective imposed severe boundaries which limited my life experiences so they would not intrude upon the fragile sense of security that we had. In addition to that, growing up in an Italian family in the 1950s in the Midwest and attending twelve years of parochial schools accentuated these limitations. This bound me to limited thinking and a diminished sense of well being as well as an inhibition of self expression. This narrow outlook created in me a sense of solitude and feelings of vulnerability.

Fortunately through my Mother's good intentions and determination, she made it possible for me to go away to college where I was able to start to think for myself and discover some sense of freedom. This was relatively short lived, however, for after I graduated I was drafted into the Army. With the Army's mandatory set of rules, regulations and discipline, I was no longer in a protected environment and felt quite vulnerable in this harsh exposure to life. However, it also brought me worldly experiences that sparked a startling awakening in me. It was there I was branded with a strong desire that could only be satisfied spiritually.

From there my spiritual awakening and journey began. I distinctly remember the moment my spiritual awakening occurred. It was in the middle of the night and I was on guard duty walking my post. I had been watching the fog roll in off the Rhine river. Then suddenly the words came to me *What am I doing here?* Right, I am in Germany on an Army base on guard duty. *However*, the *real* question that immediately emerged was *What am I doing here on earth?* It literally stopped me in my tracks and from there I took my first step onto my spiritual journey.

After many years of yoga, meditation, prayer, spiritual retreats (40 to date), reading spiritual material, and listening to spiritual teachers, a blessing occurred in my spiritual exploration through the most valuable development of channeled writing. For me, the act of channeled writing is quite simple: I allow the words I receive to come right out onto the page without my thinking about it. While it may seem mysterious, it feels completely natural to me. (I share more about Channeled Writing in the Appendix for those curious to know more.) This took place over 25 years ago, almost at the same time my first spiritual counselor stepped into my life.

Francine lived in a retirement home near where I worked at that time. She was thirty years my senior. I spent many hours with Francine. I would read her my writings and we would discuss them.

Her stern yet compassionate guidance helped me to start to open up to myself. I need to mention here that Francine was a lot more than just a counselor to me. She ended up becoming a very dear friend, my true friend. I will always cherish the friendship that we shared. I still feel her around me now even though it has been years since she has passed. She made me make a promise to her that I would always keep writing. I never broke my promise. I am including a short piece called "True Friends" in the Appendix, which I wrote twenty-five year ago to Francine.

When Francine moved away, the next spiritual counselor appeared almost at will, and then another and then another. I have spent countless hours in their patient and caring company, all with the same goal of enlightening my soul and bringing me the happiness, peace and freedom I continually seek. My writing brought me the clarity to work more productively with these kind souls.

Now, on my spiritual journey spanning five decades, I am still committed to realizing and expressing my own truth. For me, the only sure way to get in touch with myself is through writing. My writing is profound and enlightening, however, I have little to do with its content. As I let go, it just comes through. As one of my spiritual counselors once said to me, "This writing is not just for you, you know. It needs to be shared with others." It is my intention to bring you the truth that I have realized as it flows through my writing. We all deserve to be happy, which is my most passionate desire. This trilogy, you now have discovered, is a compilation of my writings, intended as a resource for you to reflect upon and to use on your own spiritual path to happiness.

THE TRILOGY'S CHANNELED MATERIAL

When I asked my last spiritual counselor where this channeled writing was coming from, she told me the source was a collective called the "Council of We." The "Council of We" is comprised of twelve nonphysical vibrational beings. Another name for them is the

"Council of the Elders" or the "Council of the Ages." They are not the wisdom itself, but instead are the Keepers of the Wisdom and they act as the ambassadors of the truth.

As representatives of this ancient wisdom – which is for humanity, the We – they impart this knowledge through a scribe; someone like me. To be of true service, a scribe interprets the knowledge they receive using their own words and makes it relatable to these current times.

I do not bring this writing through in a trance state or anything else that is exotic. My method is to be seated in a quiet environment with my journal on my lap. I put my pen and my glasses on top of my journal. I sit there in the silence and wait for the words to come. Hence the name of this Trilogy—it is literally "from quiet moments" that I receive the truth.

HOW TO ENGAGE THIS BOOK

The Trilogy is written in a question-and-answer format to bring more focus to its content. Your attention to this writing need not come from a sense of discipline or willfulness, but instead from an innate desire and willingness to know the truth and live from it. In your everyday busy life, you can sometimes be at a loss to find the time to do your spiritual practice. However, taking the time for yourself – no matter how brief – proves infinitely beneficial for you.

If it is possible, the best way to read this writing is when your mind and body are in a restful and relaxed state. For example, this can occur if you first address the body through yoga, tai chi, taking a relaxing walk in nature or spending time with your pet. Next, would be the time you spend in quiet meditation or contemplation. This can be followed by a time of prayer. Now you will be in a very receptive state to read the questions and answers so that they may seep into your mind and consciousness. This resets your mind to the truth and refreshes your soul so you can more handily meet the everyday trials and challenges you are facing. You come out more settled, more clear and ready to take action in the most powerful and proficient way.

This journey is yours and as such, leaves you to your own inner promptings. In that light this book is purposely not prescriptive. It can be read sequentially, opened randomly to any page, or skimmed to an area that catches your interest. It can be read in times of personal trauma, as a daily practice, or when you feel a need for upliftment. Take the words in these pages as they come to you – not with the intent for an intellectual understanding, but from that softer childlike part of yourself that simply wants to know.

The more you set aside a quiet time and place for yourself, the more these words will speak to you. It can be in those early hours of the morning before daily activities begin, after the kids have been put to bed, or on your daily commute to work. It does not matter. The most ideal, however, would be the sanctity of a quiet place where you can even read these words aloud; for in that way, it brings more affirmation to them.

NOTES ABOUT LANGUAGE AND GUIDANCE

Before we move ahead, a note about terminology seems in order. During the many years I journaled this channeled writing, I used various terms along the way, such as *God, Holy Father, Father, Mother Divine, Holy Divine,* the *Almighty,* the *All Knowing,* the *All Provider,* the *Creator* and so on. The word *Father* is the most comforting for me because it established for me a close and personal relationship. As you go through the materials in this book, I invite you to use the term that provides you with the most comfort and helps you establish a close and personal relationship, the way the word *Father* has done for me.

Secondly, the nature of guidance is that it gives a general answer to a specific question. The human mind is asking the question from a lower level of consciousness and what is received is an All-Knowing answer. The human mind wants to be very specific and it looks at things in a very finite way. The Divine Mind looks at things from a wider scope and an infinite perspective.

Lastly, the questions and answers included in the Trilogy came from my own practice of regular connection. As such, ideas and questions are repeated, and the repetition produces more and deeper results the more they are engaged. Results come in a subtle and gradual way. This is by design, because we humans cannot take all of this wisdom in one big gulp. We need to take it in small bites so we can digest it easily. It's like naturally talented musicians – even they need to practice, practice, practice before they get on the stage to amaze and entertain us with their unique talents and abilities.

Now I let you go on your own way and desire for you only the peace and fulfillment you are looking for.

MEETING OUR INNER DOUBTS

After reading the Introduction, you may be thinking *What am I doing? Is this really what I want to be doing right now? How do I incorporate this into my existing spiritual practice? How is this really going to help me live a more meaningful life with purpose? What if I do not understand the writing? Am I doing this right? What will my family or friends think? How will I ever find the time to do this?* This is what the mind is conditioned to do – to question and doubt – which is part of why we are here to remember something deeper than our mind regurgitations would have us know.

These are all valid questions and concerns. Yet, the bottom line is that if you are generally discontented with your life or any aspect of it, be assured that as you incorporate these questions and answers into your spiritual practice, life becomes more clear and the realizations gradually take hold and make profound changes within you. You become more self assured and act from the wisdom and strength of Spirit. In this way, you can *only* succeed. All aligns for you because you have done "the work." Is your spiritual journey without challenge? Absolutely not, however, you become more and more capable of handling what comes with grace, dignity and an assurance that you are backed by Spirit, God Himself, the Creator of all that is and all that will ever be. Remember that you are never alone and you are always being guided. It is just the matter of taking the quiet moments so you can hear the Guidance. Let's dive into the Questions and Answers your soul is seeking together now.

QUESTIONS AND ANSWERS

WHAT DOES PATIENCE GIVE US?

We must wait patiently and never despair; as we walk in the glory of our Father, we walk in strength, because we are with Him. As we meet each day head on, we revel in its glory. As we speak softly and listen intently, we exist in the moment. We must make no compromises if we desire our soul to be free. We reach to our Father in earnest, as we exchange our doubts for His comfort. We remain patient in His love and relax, knowing he is within us on our journey. Our Father's goodness surrounds us, and we have nothing to fear. As we are patient and kind with ourselves, we wake up to the glory of our Father. As we pray daily, we do not lose faith. This is our destiny. Freedom is ours.

HOW DO WE SEE THE LIGHT?

We must wake up—wake up to see the Light. We need to inspire ourselves, each and every day, and tremble no more. Our peace is now. A soft blanket surrounds us as we lie down in its peace. We do not make mention of despair. Instead, we reap our goodness and shout on high! We now surrender our soul to the Father and claim our destiny. We walk here on earth with our Father's Light in our soul. We must be a shepherd and a savior by standing in truth without waiver. Our freedom does not come easy, but the rewards reaped are dear and glorious. We wake up today to our journey, inspired as we walk hand in hand with our Father. We meet each day with His Light.

HOW DO WE GREET OUR DESTINY?

We march on, for the end is in sight. We remain calm, knowing the glory is within us. We speak softly and rejoice wholeheartedly, because we are one with all. We reach deep inside our soul and see our grace. We expose our heart to the Father. We run through the flowery meadows of our mind and lay down on the green grass of peace and calm. This is our destiny. Peace in our soul so deep, rich, and profound; no earthly trepidation can touch it. We rejoice with our whole heart and embrace the news of our godliness. We become comfortable with our identity of love and peace as we strive for its perfection at all costs. We discriminate in earnest to safely make our journey. We are refreshed today. This knowledge has set us free.

HOW DO WE SENSE HIM?

We remind ourselves daily of our strength. We doubt not our Father's love for us and we reach for Him as He touches our hand. We look up at Him and He pats our head. We listen for His soft whisper within our soul. We make Him our focus and never lose sight. We smell the fragrance of the flowers and feel His presence. We taste the honey of His love. We marvel at His greatness and bend our knee in His honor. We greet Him today with our whole heart and do not compromise one hair. We let Him well up in us. We beseech Him and are answered. We are now at One.

HOW DO WE LIVE OUR LIVES WITH PURPOSE?

We start today. As we release our desire to control the moment, the present provides miracles. Unknowing provides the opportunity to learn, and, with trust, the answers come. Our Father provides all answers. We must be confident in this knowledge. Achievements are gained by a willingness to learn. We must not be entrapped by wanting approval. We experience life's beauty in the moment as we truly accept our God-given Self. We let our false beliefs fall and trust in our unique talents and abilities. We embrace our God Self and trust the inward answers. Happiness awaits a breath away. Our true Spirit awaits us. We give into It. We follow It. We claim It. We start right now.

HOW DO WE FACE TRIALS?

It causes us great uneasiness to be forced, and we cannot shake this flagrancy. But wisdom dictates detachment, and our Father's will assures righteousness. Then, impatience rises up in us. And does this trial make us grow? Is it not there to show us our own strength? Will this awaken us to our special talents and abilities? Our confidence must be uncovered. Our awareness must be expanded. The depth of our soul must be exposed. And how will this happen? Let us see the trials of the world, then, and rely solely on our Father's love to meet them. Only with this reliance will we know the peace of detachment and let the preoccupation of thoughts be released.

HOW DO WE CREATE OUR FUTURE?

We are alert to the opportunities and listen with our heart. The future will be the present soon enough. Life presents no assurances, and they should not be sought. For where will we end up and what shall we do? The answers do not come, but the question is asked every day. Today is a gift, as is tomorrow. So we look for fulfillment today and let tomorrow come. The Father is with us always. As we are determined to listen truly from our heart, the questions end and the answers come. The future will be based on our listening today. We trust in our good fortune and expect to be lavished with His gifts. We are His child. We are blessed in our Father's solemn promise to us. We are His children and will never be forsaken.

HOW DO WE SEE OUR FATHER?

For no one can hurt us or impede our growth. We are not restricted by others, but only by our own fears. Life's greatest gifts come at our darkest hours. Our strength surges up and brings us stability and command. Our confidence may be misinterpreted, but we must not be concerned. Our destiny is to accept our gift of our true identity. We do not waver on this mission. The goal is salvation, and this road we must walk alone. As we unfold, very few will notice, but we will know. The few who do see will be happy, and the others will be frightened by our growth. The lesson is clear. Only we can drop our shackles of fear, and, in our brightness, others will follow. We must follow our destiny. Our Father's love awaits us.

HOW DO WE KNOW WE ARE NOT FORSAKEN?

We must not be afraid our Father has forsaken us. His Spirit is our essence; we cannot be apart from Him. His love for us reaches into eternity. We drink tenderly from this knowledge. We feel His peace that reigns. We walk quietly and are attentive. We are chosen by our Father. He loves His children and shares His riches. Hope is a stepping stone to our realization that our Father waits for us. He sees our struggle, and, in His love, He lets us see our strength. In this strength, we feel His presence. Then we know we are not forsaken. His love embraces us and guides us home to our place in His garden with Him.

HOW DO WE SEE INSIDE OURSELVES?

From despair, we can turn and see the light of our Father. All-loving and ever-present, He waits for us. In desperation, we seek outwardly, but when we turn inward, our life unfolds before us. We are created anew. The struggle ceases, and we flow with life's journey as peace awaits us. Patience is the key, but it warrants our diligence. Even in the dark times, we must be patient. We look for our Father in all circumstances. He leads us tenderly to happiness, peace, and knowledge of our True Self. Unpleasantness seems to surround us, but it offers opportunity. We grow, as we turn from the world to our inner Self. We are imperishable, absolute, and the pure image of our glorious Father. We are calm with the inner workings of our soul. We drop our beliefs and misconceptions and stand purely in our Father's love, which is our essence and true nature.

HOW DOES LEARNING OCCUR?

We are at ease now. We do not need to know all the answers. Through awareness, they will come. This is learning, from the inside out. This is everlasting knowledge that can never be outdated. Our intuition points us in the right direction, and we must follow it. Our awareness tells us what to do and say. As our old beliefs drop off, we spontaneously act correctly. Those who are smart in various disciplines and schooling have gained knowledge due to their intellect. We instead must believe in the knowledge that springs from us. We only use logic for the details. Our life on earth is a training ground, and on this earth plane are great opportunities for growth. We set our priorities to gain inward knowledge. We are confident in the principles we learn. These lessons are everlasting and bring us our freedom.

HOW DO WE HONOR OUR TRUE SELF?

We release the blemishes and the doubts. We look into our soul and trust its strength. The world awaits our expression; our Father bestows His talents upon us, and they must be shared with our brothers and sisters. We speak in kind words but in strength. We greet our brothers and sisters head-on, Spirit to Spirit. We do not compromise our integrity. We watch the world with its games of lies but do not fall into its lair. Our life beckons to come forth. We honor it. We let our beacon of light show forth and be a guide to bring our brothers and sisters home. We are real in our expression to them.

HOW DO WE ACCEPT OUR GOOD?

As changes come, we accept them; they are our way to the Light. We fear not the aggressors; their vision is blurred and limited. We stand up for our rights and are not afraid. The world cannot control our Spirit. We speak our mind with directness and honesty. We are anchored in our courage and have faith in our inner Spirit. As challenges arise, we accept them with confidence. We are patient with ourselves. We are filled with new confidence and courage. Our Father does not forsake us, but only grants us opportunities for growth. We are not afraid. We reach out from our soul and accept our good that awaits us. We cannot be harmed. We are steadfast. We are vigilant. We accept our true Spirit without question. Our good is at hand.

HOW DO WE BECOME MASTERS OF OUR LIFE?

Life continually comes at us, but we are of good heart. Our Father furnishes us with His tools of love and hope. Our brave heart greets today's challenges, and no worries can overshadow our day. We are sweet and kind to ourselves. We visit the place deep within our soul and rest in its peace and absoluteness. We feel our rich blessings and walk with confidence. The world holds no power over us. Independent, fresh, and forever radiant, our soul displays its true nature. We reside in the joy that our service and commitment to our Father set us free and grant us complete control over our destiny. Free from attachment, we truly love. In not seeking safety, we are secure. In not seeking validation, we are confirmed. In not wanting control, we are free. Then, we are the master of our life.

HOW DO WE DEAL WITH CONFRONTATION?

Be as it may, the search for realizations reveals unexpected results. As our comfortableness begins to fill us, we see the world again in a clear light. As we find we do not need to "be like" other people, we see them more clearly. The aim here is to be aware of the world's surroundings and manipulative attitude. Our inward vision becomes more clear and insightful. As we gain an understanding not be taken advantage of, we assert ourselves and do not manipulate for our own gain. Confrontation for manipulation's sake reflects no better than the one who intrudes upon us. Confrontation for self-realization's sake asserts our rights as a human being, and therefore espouses the truth, which is the only reality.

HOW DO WE ACCEPT THIS NEWFOUND FREEDOM?

Uneasiness arises from this newfound freedom to speak our piece, but the uneasiness we feel is not from this change, but from wanting assurances that we want it to continue. We need not worry; the seeds that were buried in the ground for so long have now given rise to these new buds of beauty and strength that have grown from within us. Enlightened by this new manifestation, we feel encouraged and more at ease. Pressure is released, and the promise of anxiety-free living whispers to us. Since life was meant to be lived in freedom, this first touch of its sweet petals enriches our soul, which has for so long wanted to be set free. Freedom cries out from within our being, and, finally, the door has started to gently swing open. May we now walk in confidence to our Father's side and make Him happy and proud that we have come home to Him. Let us rejoice in this realization.

HOW DO WE DEAL WITH THE PHYSICAL WORLD?

Let us be at peace now and settle down the rattling thoughts of others' limitations as they run through our mind. As the narrow-mindedness and density of thought stand at our door, let us announce to it that we see their presence and call their bluff. We let the anger in us rise up *and out* so it will not dampen our spirit or weigh down our day's delight. We let our intuition step forward, and our reason then follows. We sustain ourselves and validate our judgment with true perceptions from our heart and astute reasoning from our mind. Life's school teaches us many lessons and does not let us hide in routine tasks that are safe and keep us hidden.

Let it be, then, that we take up our staff and march out the door to our Father's love and blessings. We find our stiffness comfortable, because it has been around for so long. To let go brings lightness and joy. Thoughts fade away and action pours forth with ease, always producing the right results. We confront the devils within ourselves and see their reflection, as others show us large mirrors of our flaws. In our journey, as we pull out the weeds in the garden of our mind, we experience the open space to create anew. If the world, through its dark eyes and limited vision, cannot concur with our newfound freedom, it does not matter; it never will. It is only there to teach us that we can overcome its limitations. We now drop our anger toward the world's egotistic, dense view and live stronger within our own being.

HOW DO WE SEE PAST LIMITATIONS?

We are enriched today, in the truth of our own Spirit. We stand up, strong and confident. The world growls, spits, intimidates, and displays its innate need to limit all those in its path.

We become angry, fearful, and frustrated with the race consciousness, and its limited view of the world. Let us strike out in freedom today, with light in our soul, as we stand our ground, filled with our Father's love. For we seek freedom deep down within our soul. We find our answers inside ourselves, and we know the truth that awaits us there. We let the limitations of the world be, because that will never change. We let ourselves rise up to meet and accept our good. We let the richness of our soul fill us up, as we find peace in the self-expression of our inner Being. Today, we walk in peace, comforted by this truth.

HOW DO WE REALIZE THE GOOD OUR FATHER GIVES US?

The anger persists, although it has now subsided. Its tentacles hold on tightly and still create an uneasiness, but the truth spreads light over all that is troublesome. We reach inside ourselves and see the strength to let go of the dark emotion of anger, setting ourselves free to dive deeper into our soul. No emotion has power over us except the true emotion of love. We ask our Father to guide us on our journey to freedom. Let us rise up to the truth and see the shackles of negative emotions break loose and give rise to the absolute joy our Father bestows on us. We trust Him now, and as we say these words, we feel some fear and trepidation. Let us feel just a whisper of His soft touch to assure us. Let us see His hand in all creation and be one with it and Him. We resolve now even more to be free.

IS ANXIETY REAL?

Anxiety creeps in as a constant threat to our peace of mind and literally disturbs our peace. However, as we rest into it and see its true nature, we see that anxiety has no substance; it is false and empty. So as we truly try to acknowledge its existence and dive deep into it, we see it for what it truly is. We are now happy that this realization is at hand, and we use it. If anxiety plagues us, we just look it straight in the eye. We embrace it, then watch it vanish, as we go about our business and enjoy our life. The world awaits our talents to bless it. Anxiety is an obstacle to our fulfillment. We now focus on being happy today, rejoicing in our True Self. There exists our joy, which we can now share with the world.

HOW DO WE BREAK FREE?

Graciously, we step forward to our good. The lightness of Spirit touches our every breath, and we feel empowered today and blessed. Our journey has taken us far, and we rejoice in our successes.

Old patterns die hard and persist tenaciously, but our Father's undying Spirit outlives all old tendencies and inspires us to finally break free. The world continues its ways, but we reach deeper inside ourselves with the goal of total detachment. Truly, all the answers reside inside and therefore evoke proper action in the world. Duty distracts us from the words here, but we press on. Through our search, we find our salvation and break free from these earthly duties. Our Father provides for us all we need and smiles that we are finally with Him. We thank our Holy Father for our Oneness.

HOW DO REALIZATIONS COME?

But by the grace of our Father, we are revealed to our True Self. We ask, and He moves us along the path of freedom. When we stumble, He tenderly encourages our soul to endure the pain. Humbly, we beseech Him, and He provides His unending patience and support through the manifestation of His children, sent to meet us in our greatest times of need. As awareness grows, the picture becomes vastly more clear: the stumbling blocks of life placed before us were put there to make us grow and reflect upon our Father's perfect love. He watches us, infinitely more tenderly than an earthly father devoted to his children. What greater peace could we have? We are never forsaken; instead, we walk in the comfort and peace of His love and vigilance. We carry His spark of life and display it to the world in His honor. He is our life, and we are in Him.

HOW DO WE OPEN TO OUR FATHER'S MYSTERY?

It is all a mystery to us, and only through awareness does calmness arise. The wondering has limited merit and is sometimes detrimental. Worry about events not yet transpired is fruitless and drains our Father's precious energy from our soul. So we look inwardly once again, finding solace in the truth of our own omnipotence, knowledge, and assurance of His love, knowing He alone has bestowed these gifts on us and all our brothers and sisters. The time is right for us now to accept the rewards of our labors and truly accept our Father's hand on our path to freedom. From our efforts and trials, we have begun to see the light, and, from its beam, the realities of the world. So, in truth now, we realize we have control over ourselves, and the world does *not*. The mystery of life enfolds from His precious love and endearment. The world holds no value but to exercise our soul, and, in our soul's expansion, we open more to our Father's mystery.

HOW DO WE OVERCOME NEGATIVE THINKING?

Realizations come, and that is the starting point. Conditioning programs the mind and dampens the Spirit. So how will we ever finish our tasks? What do we do if "what if's" trouble our soul? Are we smart enough? Will we get it right? Will they laugh at us? Worry wrecks the mind and pummels the body with arrows of sharp points that rob it of its true functions. Poor health reflects weaknesses of the mind and the ruts of thinking it continually replays. We must stay vigilant to our inner message and see the negative thoughts for their worth. They steal our nowness and render us trapped in unhappiness. We bid them goodbye as they come now. We tell them we are not interested and go about being happy right now. This is our heritage, and our reason for being. We finally rest our soul in the assurance that we have gained the ultimate prize of our True Self.

HOW IS OUR PROGRESS MADE?

Tenderly, we walk into our long-sought awareness. As the bark falls from a tree or the skin from a snake lies behind it on the ground, we shed the old conceptions of our mind and accept the certainty of our Father's love within us. We now allow the mystery of life to unfold itself to us and walk no more in struggle, but instead in joy. We let our life take shape and go about our business with a new awareness, open to change and more confident in the power of our True Self to sustain us in all endeavors. Answers only come when we are ready, and any struggle pushes them away from our grasp. We are blessed and patient—blessed with our progress, and patient for the even greater good that will come. Life's journey is endless; there is no need to hurry down its road. Our Father offers unending abundance; there is no need to struggle to capture it.

HOW DO WE RELEASE THE FEAR?

Fear comes up, suddenly raising its ugly head. At any moment, it can storm into our consciousness, but, always, in the end it displays its uselessness. We need to be aware when it arises and settle ourselves right away, for fear's tendency is to hang on. As we walk up to it in our mind and witness its essence, we see only fog and mist; in reality, fear does not exist. It attacks our body with tension and stress and takes over, to the detriment of our body's functions.

When acting in good faith, we rely on our knowing that we have the presence to see the peace within ourselves. We have the courage to overcome all obstacles. We have the patience to wait for the right answers. We have the grace of a child of our Father. When we feel the onset of fear, we stop physically if we need to, settle into our Father's presence, and release ourselves into His love. Our happiness is there.

HOW DO WE SUSTAIN CHEERFULNESS?

We are of good cheer; our Father is always with us. No matter what we think or do, His spark remains lit within our soul. His love for us never ends, but just is. As we are enlightened to this truth, our day-to-day existence flourishes with new ideas and activities. Our untapped talents come alive, and our heart grows with His love. As we remain true to our own inner voice, we do not wander. We quiet the prattle in our mind and let our Oneness with our Father evoke its healing power into our life. It is always there, waiting for us to accept and share His grace with the world. The darkness of the world hungers for the light of the inner Spirit. The godliness in all of us waits patiently for our free will to accept it into our day-to-day lives. We must take heart that our past cannot hamper our inner Self from exposing Itself to the world.

HOW DO WE ATTAIN OUR TRUE GOAL?

Persistence toward our goal assures our success. Our true destiny is to enlighten our heart to our one True Self. The journey itself brings us tragedies and trials that we need in order to sculpt our character so our soul can shine through it. As we walk along our path, it seems long and endless, but help awaits us at every turn. Our guardian Spirit provides us the strength, encouragement, fortitude, and earthly assistance to face every challenge and endure with patience as we move forward to the goal that awaits us. Our progress is assured in our Father's presence, and love sees us through to our goal. Let us mature into a truly spiritual being, enlightened in our heart and true to our True Self. If we do that, the peace we long desire will rest forever in our bosom.

HOW DO WE ESTABLISH OUR FREEDOM?

We slip and fall, but our goal is in sight. We taste success; it nourishes us, so we press on. We move past obstacles. We are determined, resolute, and carry our passion with us; we know now that freedom is ours. We know now that we do not need to fear. We know now that we do not need to tread lightly; Our Father resides in our heart. He strengthens our soul and sends us out as His children to do his bidding. Nevermore must we enslave ourselves to doubts and fears. Nevermore must we endure despair or carry worry on our brow. We let the grace and Spirit of Him pour down upon us and touch us lightly on the forehead. We let it bring the calm and peace of its essence. We rejoice in the confidence of our successes. We profoundly declare our freedom today. We do not look back, but forward, holding to the truth of our essence. We are free today. We are forever free.

HOW DO WE STAY ON THE PATH?

Reality throws cold water on our dreams, but we dream still. We walk, relentlessly following our instincts, not our intellect. Our heart never lies to us. It walks us down the path to our true happiness. The circumstances along the way of our journey can jostle and discourage us, but we know we are on the right path. The flow of life bids us to come into it and commit ourselves without question. The world will throw its daggers at our heart, place blockades in our way, and, worst of all, play out its myriad of lies. We must be vigilant and listen to our heart's call. But we say, "How will we know?" We must be still, be confident, be patient. Our heart will not fail us. Spirit whispers to our heart. The truth is clear now. The reflection of our Being manifests through the spark of our intuition, which guides us down the path to our destiny of happiness and fulfillment.

HOW DO WE KNOW WE HAVE BEGUN OUR JOURNEY?

Our identity is more focused now. We feel the lightness of our soul and glimpse at its grandeur. The muck hangs on, but its grasp has begun to weaken. Our confidence is restored, and our journey calls us. Armed with this new knowledge, we step forth with more freedom. As we discard the old ways and throw the tension, desperation, and anxiety to the wayside, our path opens widely to the freedom we so deserve in our Father's name. The tedious, step-by-step process of turning thoughts over one by one to reveal the truth of our being has begun, and we hold our Father's hand on this journey. He comforts us and assures us of our true heritage. Finally, we realize ourselves to be of beauty, gentleness, and strength—pure in our Father Himself. We beseech our brothers and sisters to pick up their own cross and toil the fields of their minds to enlighten themselves to the happiness and freedom our Father holds for them in His heart.

HOW DO WE ASSURE OURSELVES OF VICTORY?

Beating at the door of our mind are the old ways, teeming to come back in and rest inside with their own kind. But we say no, the strength of our Father wells up in us and assures our success. To those old thoughts that have gone, we say, "Depart and wither into the nothingness from whence you came." For those that still reside, we say, "Pack our bags; your time is numbered." Awareness of the mind, released from its burdens, acts in accordance with its true nature, dictated by our Father's will, which allows godliness to reveal itself to itself and the rest of the world. Freedom reigns in our heart and strikes with its sword against the laggards that weigh it down. We must stand in truth against the spoilage of lies and fears. Our victory is assured, because glimpses of the Light inspire us to complete our journey home to our Father.

HOW DO WE MAKE OUR WAY?

Troubles try to creep back into our mind. Old thoughts hide in crevices deep inside, fearing the day when we allow our Father's Light to cast them out. The journey seems to last forever, and the progress is slow, but we feel assured as we walk up the mountain to our goal of freedom. In reality, the truth does set us free. The rest is illusion, false beliefs, and limited perception. We display the same talents, but we now see their worth. We now express our thoughts, and they are heard. We now express our feelings and are true to ourselves. Pebble by pebble, blade of grass by blade of grass, we step through our journey, assured of our victory of self-knowledge and the realization of our true Being. Nothing can stop us now—even if we stumble and fall, we are assured of success by our Father.

HOW DO WE FILL OUR SOUL?

We settle into the nature of our soul. Enriched by its blessings, we speak forth the thoughts of our heart. Blessings abound, in this newfound freedom. We act now in confidence and perform mightily, but with tenderness. We see the world's vanity, cruelty, and deceit, however, we bear witness to the truth of our soul. No fortune of gold, no fame from great deeds, no power over countries or people can measure up to the joy of our Father in our heart, confidence in ourselves, and the certainty of our faith in the eternal bliss that is our heritage. Graciously, we accept the gifts of the talents our Father has bestowed on us. We walk in the world, assured that our Father has sent us to do His work and will not forsake us.

HOW DO WE FREE OURSELVES FROM SEARCHING FOR FALSE HAPPINESS?

Sometimes, we are desperate with our fears. We want status. We want recognition. We want love. We want houses, cars, girlfriends, boyfriends, and all the traps that keep us imprisoned in our own mind. The world does not make us safe. We cannot hide away in our safe neighborhood or in our secure job. Not to know is safe. True faith is safe. Self-realization reduces and finally banishes the desires for all the worldly possessions that push away our true happiness from us. We think our happiness is always just around the corner. Instead, the answer we all quest for, that our hearts yearn for, is to be free to express our truest nature and walk in complete calmness as we display our Father's love to our brothers and sisters. Dropping desires enlightens us to the beauty and mystery of our souls and allows pure happiness to well up and pour forth.

HOW DO WE FIND TRUE SIGHT?

Be it ours, the capture of our soul. Let us reclaim its warmth and rekindle the flame of the true life we now embark upon. Our spirit soars with the joy of its freedom. We realize now the folly of false pursuits and desires that took us down the wrong path. Enlightened by our victories of realization of what is, we drop our old conventions and bring ourselves into the moment. The sharp edge of emotions dulls slightly, and hope presses us forward on our journey. We stay vigilant, as the ego attempts to claim victories and tries to present itself as superior. We rest in the truth and the clarity that brings us to our inner sight. We are blessed to have this gift bestowed upon us. Our heart becomes more at peace, and we find comfort in knowing, discarding the ignorance we once had. Let us walk this hard road that gives us this sight.

HOW DO WE RECOGNIZE OUR BLESSINGS?

Blessed be the Spirit within ourselves. The essence of ourselves waits for us while it sits in eternity. Manufactured beliefs, fractured emotions, stress, and strain cover it from our sight. Blessed be our awakening. As us peel off the burdens of our mind, our body relaxes into a healthier state. Our mind becomes more clear, and our days come to greet us. Blessed be our heart. It feels the richness of love and shares itself more freely. Our patience grows, and contentment rests where struggle once ruled. Blessed be our relationships. The sharp edge of agitation has dulled, and friendly interchange flows, guided by our new understanding. Blessed be our Father, who grants us all these gifts. His mightiness, tenderness, and illumination sustain the spark of life and brilliance we shine out upon the earth. Blessed be our Father as we praise Him.

HOW DO WE ALLOW SPIRIT TO COME FORTH?

We let the spirit of our Father deep inside our soul guide us to our journey's end. Blessed by illumination, we navigate our way home. Once the veil is lifted, life rushes in fully. It does not come with a thunderous wave, but with a light caress, so sweet that we bow down before it. Majestic and oh-so-beautiful are the heights our awareness has reached! But this is just the beginning; our Father lays out for us our true work now. Our trials have prepared us for the tasks at hand. Our enlightened soul can now reach out in peace to its fellow brothers and sisters and whisper the truth to those who seek it. We are proud of overcoming our challenges, and we walk with distinction, remaining humble in our work. He who sent us showers us with His blessings and lavishes His love upon us. We must be vigilant and always honor the source of our Being. Then, and only then, will we truly experience the happiness and tenderness our Father bestows on all of us.

HOW DO WE FIND THE HAPPINESS WE SEEK?

Progress brightens our life and makes our way easier. Life has more fluidity, and resolutions pour into us. Attempting to construct our life is fruitless, however, living our life is a gift. Old ways linger on but are losing their foothold. So we walk taller. We look ahead. We witness our life changing. We feel relieved and happier. This is the true goal. The gift of a true life is more precious than the finest gem, more sweet than the purest honey, and more powerful than the ruler of a great nation. We bend our knee in prayer and thanksgiving, and, in the same breath, we ask for more happiness and everlasting peace. Our Father provides us an infinite spring of happiness that never runs dry. We drink in His life as much as we are able, and we yearn for Him. His gift is endearing and completely unselfish. It does not distinguish between beggar or king, sick or healthy, destitute or rich. All he asks of us is to want Him, to need Him, to worship Him above all else. We praise Him and feel our peace. He rests inside us.

HOW DO WE MAKE THE CHOICE TO LOVE OUR FATHER, ALONE?

We ask You to take away the hurt and fear, dear Father. We walk along this long path and wonder where the journey ends. We sometimes grow tired, or is it our patience that needs to be exercised? But only we can drop these burdens. You give us the tools to lift up our soul. You give us the help to guide us along the way. We alone must decide our own fate. When our hands hurt so and our back tires from carrying the weight, only then do we cry for Your help. So we wait in Your everlasting patience and love. When we decide to wake up to You, our heart lightens and burdens drop from our arms. We can walk more erect now. We can see more clearly. The heavenly grace and light of Your love fill us. So let us move down the path and release these burdens. Let us make the choice once and for all, to devote ourselves fully to You. Then will we realize the freedom we yearn for.

HOW DO WE FIND YOU, FATHER?

Let us give thanks just for today, just for this moment. In truth, that is all we have. We feel our inner soul reaching out to express itself, and in that yearning, we find relaxation and calm. It brings us into the present, and every impulse and inspiration comes from deep inside us. We cannot begin to count our blessings, because there are so many. So when our own desires get in the way, we stop and drop back into the moment, feeling calm and peace come over us. We let the inner vision of our heart see out, and the clarity startles us with the amazement of the blessings we possess. We see each day with a new vision. As we take our steps upon this earth, we walk with dignity and the knowledge that we have seen the Promised Land in our mind and heart. Let the world not bind us down. We reach into the moment for our peace, which awaits us there. Then, as the moments flow into each other, we step into the eternity of our True Self realized.

HOW DO WE REALIZE YOUR MIGHTY GIFT TO US?

Fear continually knocks at the door of our mind. It is easy to let it in, where it takes over and causes turmoil and uncertainty. We now become stronger and turn our mind toward our infinite source. We take hold of thoughts of the our Father, who immediately comforts us. We turn our mind from anguish to resolve, our heart from despair to hope, and our body from cringing to the reality of its true nature of health and vitality. So things did not go right today, and, at times, we felt uncomfortable or worried. These are just passing moments, like leaves riding on a breeze. We root ourselves now, in the reality of the glory of our Father. We proceed in courage and strength, because that is who we are. We are confident and know our Source. It is unchanging and absolute in its essence. Our Holy Father comforts us in our trials. He sees us when we falter and cringe, as the mask of fear shows its face. Let us continue to remember our heritage, as pure, absolute, unwavering, and so profoundly blissful and powerful that no man, circumstance, or feeling can shake it or cover it up. We live in peace and grace.

HOW DO WE MANIFEST OUR SOUL?

Rest assured, we will meet our goals. As we dive into the depths of our soul, we enjoy a freedom so fresh that its manifestation cannot be smothered or covered up. Our heart sings with the joy of freedom, as we move slowly into the knowledge of our True Self. We all walk upon this earth in search of the enlightenment of our soul, which holds the gift of our talents. Even those so fortunate to display their wares are eager to explore and expand on the many gifts bestowed upon them. We transform our mind to see the light that exists in all things. The struggles we bear give us the opportunity to overcome, grow, and shed our light out into the world. We drop the weight of worry and self-consciousness and step out into the real life that awaits us. There are great risks, but the reward is the freedom of our heart and the manifestation of our soul.

HOW DO WE GAIN OUR FREEDOM?

We banish this devil of fear we have overcome and now walk free. The light shines upon our path, and we step with confidence into our destiny. The lingering threads of doubt try to hang on, but we cut them with the confidence of a warrior who knows the battle he has won. Our journey beckons us to the fulfillment we yearn for deep within us. Let us shake the remaining sadness and pondering of insecure thoughts that still linger. The fine line of arrogance and confidence, we must walk; we are bound now to our Father and His will. We proceed in our life with the unending rhythm of the waves, the natural turn of the seasons, and the cycle of the sun, beginning and closing each day. The peace we yearn for has settled in our heart, and we bathe in its sweet embrace. We give thanks for what we have and who we are. We look at each other equally and bow down in worship to our Father, who provides us our soul, His peace, and the very essence of ourselves.

HOW DO WE ACCEPT OUR FATHER'S GRACE?

Let us not fear again. We walk to our Father, His arms open to greet us. His heart sings with the joy of His love that we have finally come home to Him—home in His arms, home by His side. We have yearned so long for this moment, and now, finally, we rest in the peace of our Father's gift of heaven to all of His children. No longer must we doubt, fear, or struggle with the insecurities that bound our soul and smothered our heart. Our innate calling spurs us on. Our yearning to breathe in our new life settles our soul and establishes the promise of joy, where doubt once stood. So now, at this time of triumph, we give thanks and relax into the grace our Father has bestowed on our heart and mind. Let us move in confidence, compassion, and the absolute knowledge that we are our own person, grounded in our Father's love. Let our Father's light guide our every thought and fill us with His grace.

HOW DOES FORGIVENESS FREE US?

Let our spirit sing out and rejoice. Let our Father's light show forth upon our path. Let our faith guide us and enrich and comfort our soul. The evils and transgressions of the world seek to destroy our spirit and weaken our heart. We stand now in strength and look ahead to our good fortune. Through the lessons of life, we learn of our own strength and break off the illusions and falsehoods that try to encircle our mind. For those that trespass against us, we do not falter; they cannot harm our Spirit and steadfastness to reach our journey's end. We forgive those who wallow in their weaknesses and move toward our destiny. We see the reality of this world and turn to embrace in our heart the reality of our Father's heritage He bestows upon us. So now we let go of the bad deeds beset on us and release them. They have no power over us or our progress toward enlightenment.

HOW DO WE COME HOME TO OUR FATHER?

Fear reaches deep inside us and holds on tightly. It has become comfortable and complacent. It has enjoyed its home. We are starting to wake up, however, and this annoys it and threatens its grip. We vow now to overcome it and release it from our thoughts and feelings. We feel more confident and powerful every day. We progress with small steps that now expand into great strides. Our heart is fixed on the truth that we were born to be free. As we continually turn to our Father and feel His almighty strength in our heart, we can only succeed. We are confident and assured of our success. Outward signs still linger, and old habits pull us down the same old roads of doubt and fear, but we grow stronger every day. We walk with more assurance. We start to see the light in our soul and are happy with ourselves, our True Self. We must walk with our Father; without Him, we are lost. As fear ruthlessly tries to tighten its grip, we say no more, no more.

HOW DO WE STRENGTHEN OUR RESOLVE?

Our life expands now. We reach for our freedom, which opens up its arms to us. Our heart, enveloped with our Father's love, sings with liberation. The long years of doubt, worry, and fear are cracking. They will soon drop off and no longer weigh down our mind and body. The sweet taste of life, true life, whets our desire for more of its abundance. Old patterns die very hard, but determination and perseverance hand us our victory. Our faith allows us to walk forward. Our

Father's love provides us the strength to continue. We are assured of victory. Our footing has become more solid. A smile comes easier to our face. Others' knowledge no longer intimidates us, but instead encourages our mind's curiosity to explore even further. Life's greatest challenge lies before us. We accept our Father's gift, which allows us to resolve our insecurities, accept ourselves, and walk with the confidence and assurance of ourselves realized. We vow to accomplish this goal, with the help of our Father.

HOW DO WE DROP OUR LIMITATIONS?

Admissions bring freedom, and then the work must begin. Our faults die hard; their roots reach deep into our mind. However, our determination to eradicate these intruders stands everlasting, resolute, and courageous. Our happiness depends upon us. The sorrows in our life weigh more heavily than they need to. Blessings that come in the subtlety of thoughts embolden us. We vow to walk in dignity, self-sufficiency, and happiness. Our holy Father's intention allows us to realize the love within us, buried by our faults of discouragement, uncertainty, and valuing others opinions of ourselves. We promise ourselves a victory by the release of our admissions and the dark secrets that entangle our soul. Through our Father's almighty power and His infinite faith in our innate abilities, we now walk in freedom and respect as we realize the truth within ourselves.

HOW ARE WE INSPIRED ON OUR JOURNEY?

Our inspiration to find ourselves comes from our knowing deep in our soul that the Promised Land lies within us. A journey outward is fruitless in the search for freedom and cherished happiness. When we follow our True Self, we find great peace. We move ourselves toward this truth. We long to be true to ourselves, without reservation or any self-righteousness. Our progress inspires us to press on and overcome the seeming stream of obstacles and traps that lie in waiting. Oh, but as we shed light on ourselves, the mountains give way to tiny pebbles we can easily walk over. The strength and wisdom of our Father enlightens us. So the lesson is to allow, not force the progress. Nature slaps us in the face when we go it alone, but our Father lifts us up and carries us through it all. All we need to do is watch.

HOW DO WE SEE OURSELVES AS OUR FATHER DOES?

As we come into our peace, we realize the simplicity of it. Our life's journey brings us down this road of realizations. Our real world resides right in front of our eyes, but we have not seen it. Old habits and beliefs robbed us of our happiness. Now, our life abounds in blessings and love we have created. As we crawl out of the hole of darkness that rested in our mind, we see the true light that has always surrounded us. The blessings of our life astound us and make us weep with thanksgiving, as we now experience the joy that has been buried deep in our heart. Old habits and thinking deter our journey into the Light and still hang on with ferocity, but determination and the will of our Father in reality are the victors. Faith is the answer, as we exercise absolute belief in our Almighty Father and resolute faith in ourselves and the power that lies within us. Determination is our ally to reach the goal of the reality of ourselves. Perseverance is our sword in all trials that try to trap and ensnare us and stop us from the destiny of our heritage. These virtues stand at our bidding to pick up and use according to our Holy Father's will and laws.

Deviations come easy as successes are achieved; the ego waits in the dark crevices of our mind to guide us back into destruction. So we must be vigilant as well as humble for the gifts that our Father bestows upon us, His blessed children. We walk with dignity, not egotistical pride. We are thankful for our bounty. We share our Father's gifts with others but do not trick ourselves into thinking in any way we are superior. We all share in the gracious, loving Spirit of our Father as equals, one to another, spreading His love, grace, and goodwill. May we be at peace with these heavenly gifts of realization that enlighten us.

HOW DO WE KEEP FROM BEING DISCOURAGED?

We need not be discouraged with the trials and setbacks of life. Progress comes through mistakes, heartaches, and pure determination. We let our faith sustain us and our heart guide us to our goal of fulfillment and peace. Our Father never forsakes us, but instead stands ever-ready to pour forth His love into our life. We need to stay the course and focus on our Spirit and the inner workings of our heart. The ups and downs of life will come and go, but our faith, honesty, and love for ourselves last forever. So we press on in this worldly life, and focus on the true realities of our soul and mind. The sustenance of our Father's love pours over us with abundance and everlasting care, sustaining our well-being. We drop the illusions of the world and step into the happiness and glory our Father provides for us. We accept it *now*.

HOW DO WE THROW OFF THE PAST?

We need not be not ashamed of any past mistakes. This trap of guilt and pride hides the very light of our soul. We press on to walk freely. We drop the stones that weigh down our mind and heart. We breathe in the Spirit of our Father and walk with the dignity and bearing of His child. The trials are many, and traps abound to ensnare us or cripple us into despair. We resolve to be faithful until the last. We resolve ourselves to love our Father without reservation. As we use discernment, this will make us even wiser. The simplicity of life is there for the taking. It stands, ready to rest in our heart. We let it be. We accept our heritage. We throw off the pain from the past and let the future meet the present and no longer intrude on the happiness that awaits us right now. We accept ourselves right now, and our life resounds with happiness.

HOW DO WE CLAIM OUR VICTORY?

Our spirit sings with joy and lightness. We feel our soul breathing easily. We give thanks for all our blessings. Life's journey seems unkind, and sometimes cruel. Our heart is enriched with the thought of our Father's love for us. We trust ourselves now, and watch sometimes daunting circumstances resolve themselves. We pray for the peace of our Father to ease our mind and we relinquish the hard thoughts of worry and discouragement that have plagued us. Our destiny of fulfillment, joy, and happiness beckons us. Our answer of resolve, determination, and patience guarantees our conclusion of unending peace in our Father's arms. We are happy today, in our thoughts that we are forever loved. We look to the gift of faith to carry us through to the end. We walk proudly in the realization of our assured victory.

HOW DO WE CLAIM OUR FREEDOM?

Old feelings hang on, but we must be persistent. We tell them to stop and go away. We pull these weeds from our mind and leave them behind us. Our real life of joy and abundance awaits us. We smile gently to ourselves and truly know the love our Father holds for us in His heart. Only we can drop the ravages of the past and step forward into our new freedom. We stop letting life's stumbling blocks weigh down our mind, but instead ride the ever-changing waves of life. We stand erect and tall, and feel our self-worth rise from within us. The preciousness of self-love frees our mind and heart. We see ourselves as our Father sees us—aware, alert, and focused on our true identity; we are really Him. We are His child, and His love pours over us. We feel it, embrace it, and let it be our own. This is the simple truth of it: our Father and His children in everlasting joy and love.

WHAT MUST WE DO TO SUCCEED?

We are on our own. Only we can rise to our everlasting freedom. The kind hand of true friends helps us along the way, but in truth, it is our own choice. Determination, perseverance, and faith in ourselves carry us to the end. The finish line of life is only the beginning of the joy that awaits us. Our assessment of our own deeds stands as our only judge. We take heart that it is ourselves that have complete control of our life. Our decisions dictate our consequences and reflect back to us the very thoughts we hold deep in our heart. So we lighten our load, raise our chin, and look at the good that surrounds us now. Our blessings can only multiply and grow in our heart. The peace of our Almighty Father sustains us, and our faith in ourselves aligns us to this truth. We rest now and enjoy our peace.

HOW DO WE RELEASE THE OLD WAYS?

We cause our own emotions from our thoughts. We see ourselves causing our own anxieties and perpetuating our fears. No one has control over us but ourselves. This new awareness of watching ourselves is a wake-up call to our opportunity to admit we cause our own problems. We now banish these old ways and pick up the torch of our true life, which lights our way. Judgment has no place here. Love rules, and through its perception, the way unfolds to eternal happiness, which only expands upon itself. We admit our mistakes. Our blindness blocks the light, which shows the way. We vow, day by day, to move on to the green pastures of life and lie down among the beautiful flowers our Father has laid out there to grace our heart. Freedom calls us, and we now listen. The wandering in the desert has ended.

HOW DO WE ASSURE OURSELVES?

Riches await us, and they stretch out their arms to welcome us. Our soul aches for the everlasting presence of peace that surely reigns in our heart. The blessings of nourishment and support comfort us on our way to the freedom we seek and will achieve. Miracles flood into our life; at every turn, we are supplied with all our needs along our journey. We now walk to meet our demons and face their fierce battle to hold us down in the mire of illusions, doubts, and fear. We bring a fresh determination to our task and pick up our sword of valor. Aided by the gentleness in our heart, we now overcome the mighty Goliath with assuredness, calm, and confidence that devours the smoke-filled recesses of our mind. Clarity now lights our way, and we stand, erect and strong. We press on through our Father's guidance and see His hand resting on our shoulder. It has always been there.

HOW DO WE EXPERIENCE HEAVEN?

The realities of our Father's love seep into our mind when we let them. We are on our own here. Our free will is truly that. We do control our own destiny; that is our true nature. Through allowing ourselves the freedom we so have long desired, we crack the boundaries of our mind, and the light shines through like the sun filtering into a cave. Faith has carried us to this point and sustained us in our darkest hours. We now move on, and let the fractured rocks of old beliefs crumble at our feet. The glory is absolutely our Father's, but we now allow it to shine its Light on and through us. Only in this way, can we rest and be at peace. So we let the healing continue and walk ever so slowly. As nature recreates itself, so must we. We follow our heart, and it leads us to our True Self, which has always been there, waiting for us. This is our Father's gift to us—Himself. This is heaven.

HOW DO WE WAKE UP?

We relax into our own strength and feel its vitality well up within us. Our power is God-given, and we claim it now. We use it wisely to navigate the world on our own terms. This is our heritage, and we accept it. The illusions of our mind have masked our self-worth, but now we pull away the cobwebs of despair and fright and redeem ourselves. Our journey is just beginning into our new world of love and self-confidence. We see the dullness in people's minds and walk away. Our triumphs must come from hard work. We are willing to continue on to free ourselves from the bindings of others' thoughts and walk into our realization of our True Self. We vow to drop the smelly sacks of garbage in our mind that we have carried for so long. We promise ourselves and our Father a victory, fueled by determination and accompanied by His love.

WHAT DOES OUR JOURNEY BRING US?

We stand before You, Father, and in the light of Your love we finally realize the peace we long have sought. Our heart beats easier now, and our breath eases itself. Our mind has spun webs of confusion and disharmony on a train that has gone nowhere. As we reach into our soul for the answers, we find them there. Our way is made clear now; all we need to do is walk on our path to our freedom. Each illusion we drop brings us closer to the realization of our Father within us. It waits there in eternity for us to come home to it. Our Spirit calls to us, and we must answer it. Our life begins now in its true reality; before, we were only wandering. Our riches await us, but we must be patient. The trappings of our old life hang on, and we must discard these old rags and claim our rewards of eternal life with our Father. Our success is assured.

HOW DO WE CONQUER THE LAST OF IT?

The tension builds in us because we let it. The anger persists, but its residue is now weak. It is losing its control as our awareness and strength take its place. The last fort to be captured seems daunting and impossible, but we still press on. The gentle soul we are emotes strength, dignity, and purpose. The world cannot intrude on us unless we let it. So let us come to terms with the reality of our own creations, and let us see the light that shines on and in us. We must reach for this light; it is truly us, and any other perception is false and must be discarded in its entirety. Our hesitancy and lack of self-confidence have been programmed into us; their roots run deep and have covered our soul for a very, very long time. We see this clearly now, and with patience and love, we conquer it.

HOW DO WE REALIZE THE RICHES OF OUR LIFE?

The riches of life await us now, and we see them now. They sparkle like the sun's rays on ruffled waters. Their glimmer beckons us, as we stand on the shore of our own consciousness. The realities of the world sharpen our awareness, and in turn, we see more of what the world offers us. Its lessons light up our soul, which allows us to walk with more freedom. Our heart aches for our true destiny, but that will not bring it to us any sooner. Strength, courage, determination, gentleness, patience, and love unravel the knotted tapestries of our mind and set it free to ponder the beauty that lies within our very soul. So we continue on our journey, resisting the temptation to look back and paralyze ourselves with regrets, resentment, and self-pity. We abandon our need to control the events in our life and instead rest our mind in the wonderment of the moment that offers us its riches without reservation.

WHAT CHANGES NEED TO OCCUR IN OUR LIFE?

The bounty of riches flows into our soul and heart, filling the emptiness that once echoed with a lack of direction and purpose. Our life reflects a transition from insecurity and wanting to undisciplined expression, calmness, and then self-assurance. The skin of unhealthy beliefs and habits sheds itself and displays the truth we have long searched to find within ourselves. We watch the change and rest easy in our progress of unfoldment to a true life of unbounded expression. The journey appears long, but, in reality, transpires in the blink of an eye. Our reward of eternity brightens a light within us that dissolves any darkness of struggle. Now we rejoice, as we take our remaining steps to the "Land of Milk and Honey." For any appearance of doubt, uncertainty, or threat is just that. There is no greater reward than the happiness of the truth of our Father, self-realized in our very soul.

HOW DO WE LIVE IN THE SIMPLICITY OF LIFE?

The spark of our Father's light eases our weary soul. It nurtures us, as we draw our attention to its essence. Our deepest awareness reflects to us our True Self. The clarity of the moment releases us to simply be. We observe life while we act in true accordance with our Father's laws. Abundance comes from total surrender to our Father's desires, as our Father only wants true happiness for us. So we shall seek and find Him. We shall knock, and He will open the door to us. We shall enter His Kingdom. We shall rejoice in His glory. We shall rest in the knowledge of our True Self and gain the reward of everlasting peace, which can never be destroyed, because it simply is; all else is illusion.

HOW DO WE STRENGTHEN TRUST IN OURSELVES?

Our spirit grants us all the strength and fortitude we need. We just need to ask for it. We drop our pride and self-pity. We look deep into our soul and swim in the infinite reservoir of unending love and nourishment, which is ourselves. It is our True Self that whispers softly to us, which we only hear when we drop the chatter that churns in our mind. We falter in our old ways and bruise our knee once again against the sharp rocks of self-doubt and its brother, anxiety. But then we rise again, and when we do, we walk a little more freely than we did before. We find strength in our own fortitude. We find more resolve with each step. We stand more strong and erect. We become more firm in purpose. We see our goal of freedom more clearly and continue on toward it. This is our purpose. This is who we really are.

HOW DO WE RELEASE LIMITING THOUGHTS?

As we lighten the load of our mind, our heart sings out in happiness. The fodder of worry and projection of fear weigh down our soul with unnecessary hardship. The tools of fear weave webs of uncertainty, and lack of focus in our action. Our energy is squandered on the churning of illusions that play themselves in our mind. Let us be vigilant of our thought patterns and watch them create the circumstances of our lives. We experience the outcome of our thoughts, good and bad, as they play out before us in the physical world. So now we choose the road to our freedom, which offers peace to our mind, strength to our soul, and lightness to our heart. We must abandon the pattern of thoughts and feelings that have dictated our lives with the theme of not being worthy or good enough. We must abandon thoughts of "*they* are going to get us." We must abandon thoughts that we will never have the happiness we want. We must abandon the refuse that has preoccupied our minds over so many years. We must claim our peace right now, in this very moment. We let it be so.

HOW DO WE NAVIGATE THIS ROAD TO OUR FREEDOM?

The road to freedom winds with many turns. The goal seems elusive, but in reality, it sits restfully, waiting to be realized. Only by awareness can we avoid the pitfalls, snares, and illusions that attempt to delay our progress. The change from long-established patterns of thoughts to living a new reality of true life and love of ourselves comes at a high cost. Yes, the road is not easy, but its rewards are great and eternal. So how do we walk down the road we started as a small child, trapped in a physical body of a young person? How do we walk down the road as an adolescent trapped in the body of a middle-aged individual? We walk with the power of determination and dignity. We walk with the power of self-love. We dive into our being so deep that we resound to the world our True Self. We vow to have our freedom and a life filled with plenty and abundance. We continue on our road and watch the signposts point us to everlasting peace. We become self-realized, self-assured, and evoke the purity of the child of our Father. We stand erect and strong in the freedom that emanates from our being.

WHAT IS OUR TRUE GOAL IN LIFE?

The grip of time spent in unhealthy patterns appears foreboding, but in reality, it does not exist and has no power. The mind binds itself up and tricks itself into thinking there is no way out. The ego prompts the mind to do its bidding, and the ego promotes itself as the only answer and salvation to our problems. Our Father stands in the wings and waits for our cry for help. Only when we turn our attention away from our selfishness and truly drop our desire for self-gratification and false goals does our Father help us. Pure, unadulterated devotion to our Father and unwavering determination to save our soul are the only answer to eternal redemption. Every rock must be turned over. Every wrong must be forgiven.

Every mistake must be loosened and dropped from our mind. Every feeling of self-doubt or low self-worth must untie its noose from around our heart. We must remember that in reality we have no control over anyone else's decisions or destiny. Each soul must find its own peace in its own way. Any interference or manipulation entraps us in our own insecurities. So we take heart in the truth that our Father, the Almighty, loves us with such tenderness that, if we knew, we would weep with joy for eternity. Our very breath now relaxes with this thought. So we continue to be steadfast and drop the old ways that bind us to the earth plane, in drudgery and ill-content. We stop our search for outward signs of happiness, lay our weary souls in the bosom of our Father's love, and rest there in eternity. This is our heritage. This is our only goal.

WHAT IS OUR TRUE REWARD?

Our mind stumbles again, but we see it now as it falters. We watch it step over the rough cobblestones of built-up sludge and waste, hardened from years spent in worry and self-pity. Ah! As the light begins to show dimly through the crevices of new belief, hope springs from our heart. Our way is clear, although we must still walk it. Life *does* offer its bounty to those who search their souls in honesty and lay themselves bare before our Father. The true miracles come in small packages, hidden from view from those who choose a worldly path. Our Father graciously granted us free will, and in that act, He lights the spark of Himself in all beings. So we make our choice to walk back to our Father and meet ourselves there in His outstretched arms. We now reach deep inside to our True Self and watch all the falsehoods drop off like snow falling from branches in the dawn of spring. We set foot on the golden carpet our Father has laid out for us, His children. We rejoice in our good fortune. We have honored and respected our Father, and He has shown Himself to be us, and us Him.

WHAT IS THE TRUTH OF OUR EXISTENCE?

We feel tremendous relief when the burdens of erroneous thoughts begin to dissipate and lose their power and control. A life spent in the dungeon of feelings of inadequacy and lack of self-confidence begins to come to a close. The rich life of the choice of all possibilities opens its golden gate as it calls to us. Its scent warms our souls, and its comfort fills us up with a soft happiness and joy. We are the charters of our own destiny. This responsibility need not weigh heavy, but must be realized; in this awareness, freedom floods over and in our very souls. We are meant to struggle and grapple with the problems that face us. This causes the Spirit to rise up and recognize itself. This cognizance validates our true existence. In this knowledge, we know we are. We exist in eternity.

HOW DOES AWARENESS ENLIGHTEN US?

As awareness rises, it reveals the present moment with more clarity and dissolves artificial boundaries. Past events come into focus, shedding light on the reasons why turmoil existed and how it was created. No blame exists here. It just is or was that way. Devoted attention to our Father opens the door of our mind, lightens our heart, and frees our soul. By the measure we devote ourselves to being aware, our reward will be received. Distractions abound, bombarding our senses to the point of dullness, so we search for more to satisfy our desires. This downtrodden path brings us to a dead end of failures and emptiness. Awareness simply turns on the light in the dark rooms of our mind, and lets us walk in freedom instead of banging us against the hard edges of our life. No need exists anymore to hurt ourselves through ignorance and the darkness that caused us such devastating blindness. Our Father has granted us the gift to choose our own way, and as we decide to walk back to Him, He enlightens us from our false beliefs and old bad habits. We become more aware of our Father residing in us. Our Father's existence is closer than our very breath.

WHERE IS OUR RESTING PLACE?

A restless soul must come to terms with its perceived shortcomings. The life of any human being affords us many opportunities to grow into our True Self. The bounty of freedom waits in a restful tranquility until we claim it. It does not come knocking on our door; it resides in our house already. To meet the challenges of life head-on dissolves the turmoil instantly and lays down a path directly to the sea of freedom residing patiently within us. Each fear, whatever its form, must be entered into, confronted, and given its boot out the door. The only thing remaining in our house must be us. When we realize ourselves, we realize our freedom. We realize our true power. We realize unbounded possibilities to express ourselves, free from inhibitions that we let our ego impose upon us. So we then simply relax in our own house.

HOW DO WE BEST SERVE OUR BROTHERS AND SISTERS?

When we truly touch our soul, we realize the pearl in the depths of ourselves. We realize the world operates from the inside out, and not the outside in. We realize our destiny lies in our own hands, and no one else's. At that point, life opens up to us, its arms stretched wide. We experience grace in our thoughts and actions. Others begin to take notice and start knocking on our door. In a true, loving spirit, we give them bricks to carry as they come; to those we love more, we give a larger and heavier stone. We know, only through honest effort and determination, rewards reveal themselves. Therefore, we pass out challenges of life to our brothers and sisters, who search for their way. The devious walk away. The weak drop the heavy load and look elsewhere to fill themselves. The novices question, but take to their tasks in faith. The strong ask for more to carry. In the end, we can only sit at each other's table in true friendship if we carry our own load.

HOW DO WE REALIZE OUR DESIRED RESULTS?

The reality of ourselves opens up a deluge of possibilities, only limited by our own imagination and the determination to set out on a desired path. As awareness expands upon itself, we watch the creation of our world unfold before us. At this stage, discernment plays a major role in our growth process as the realization sets in that life mirrors back to us our very thoughts put into action. We must decide with great care the fate we now take into our own hands for ourselves. No gift or reward can be denied to us if we set out our mind to a specific end. The natural order of life rushes in to support and sustain us at every step of our chosen goal. Life's ultimate gift is the giving of itself, and when we allow ourselves to receive it with complete faith and trust, its presence within us fills us up to such a point that words pale next to it and simply wither away. Stepping onto the stage of self-realization starts a new journey into a full life, where before we only existed.

WHAT DOES EACH DAY TELL US?

At last, we stand with firmer footing, as the storms of the day wash onto the shores of our mind. Any attempt to shake us falters more than it did the day before. Realizations result in clarity, strength, confidence, and a relentless fortitude. Every inch gained reflects the effort of every thought turned and every action taken. One must walk the internal journey alone; no one else can carry us forward. If they did, it would rob us of our very soul. So we let the day come and bring with it what it will. Any attack against us will strengthen our spirit and make us wiser. Every surprise will bring sweet joy. Command of ourselves brings with it utter contentment and peace, which encourages those who are searching for their own way. The cloudy minds of the unaware do not see us. The cruel souls hunt elsewhere for their spoils. The beauty of the day lightens up to greet us, and we rest in ourselves. Peace does exist.

HOW DO WE SEE OUR ONENESS WITH OTHERS?

The grace of our Father's loving hand gently touches our shoulder. In that moment, our breath stops, in awe of the power that fills us. Absoluteness surrounds us, rests inside us, and we fold back into it. It is us. No separation exists. This fallacy was created by minds of those men that cannot see beyond themselves. Separation implies fear and a constant struggle to protect oneself. This misconception causes families to split, communities to battle crime, and nations to shed the blood of young men and women. Only through the search of oneself can the madness of the world cease. Each man, woman, and child must decide for themselves their own fate. We each hold in our hands the very essence of who we are. In that realization, we see that all mankind is ourselves. Yes, it is absolute. We are one.

HOW DO WE REALIZE THE BEGINNING OF OUR AWAKENING?

At last, the peace begins to settle into our mind. The chatter dims itself, because the ground has been tilled and the good soil now rests on top. The feeling of assuredness enters us, where once no room existed. Although we continue on our journey, the burdens that weighed us down no longer cut deep into our shoulders. We reap the rewards of the new buds that begin to sprout, and we water them with the tenderness and truth we see within ourselves. Life opens its arms to us, and we walk to meet it. We are glad we are alive to see the dawn of this day. We step through the door of darkness into the light. Its grace urges us on to ever bigger rewards that we will discover inside ourselves.

HOW DO ACCEPT LIFE'S GIFTS?

Freedom's bell rings in our hearts, and we dance eagerly to its chime. We sing out in harmony with the universe, which shows us its rhythm and beauty. A small bird lands gently and begins its search for food, as we watch in wonder. Nature's hand nurtures it and provides an unending supply of comfort. So we continue on and begin to accept our place, as nature pours out its bounty upon us. As the bird searches for food, so must we engage life to bring us our honored gifts. As we drop life's troubles, our hands are free to pick up life's joys.

WHAT IS THE WAY TO COEXISTENCE AND FREEDOM?

Our spirit wells up in us and cannot be denied itself. The flow of awareness brings with it the natural order of things. Trust in ourselves shines a bright light outward that spontaneously displays right choices and brings rewards without the toil of struggle. Our happiness begins to bubble up, and it does not send rockets into the air, but instead provides us a steadier hand to command our lives. We all possess the very same nature to be free, but only in claiming freedom *can* we be free. True love allows coexistence as well as freedom. Domination and passivity have no place in harmony. Harmonious freedom portrays an even flow of our Father's will. Our Father's will can only give, and in giving, it receives unto itself. The profound intelligence of nature displays the delicate balance of the harmony of life. When we surrender to our True Self, we allow the flow of our Father's will to resonate in our lives, and coexistence occurs naturally. Love attracts love and cannot be denied itself.

HOW DO WE REALIZE OURSELVES?

Happiness abides in us, and its manifestation displays the truth within ourselves. As we allow our steps to take hold in our lives, we realize the very nature of life itself. Stepping into life allows us to reach more into ourselves. As we continually reach into ourselves, we make stronger and longer strides into life. So only by agreeing to be ourselves do we truly live. This is the truth; no other way exists.

WHAT IS THE TRUTH ABOUT DEATH?

Death's only claim resides in an illusion that we no longer exist. As man leaves the earth plane, his existence still resides in the hearts and minds of those he touched. His Spirit resides in a new level of existence, from which he sends the same love he did while he was upon earth. So the spirit and love of a man for his dear ones and friends knows no space or time. It is eternal. Therefore, it cannot ever be lost.

HOW DO WE ENDURE THE STRUGGLES OF LIFE?

The gift of our Father reveals itself to us only when we search in earnest, honesty, and with complete focus. No room exists for any other thoughts or intentions. Gradually, our true lives and our True Self open up to us, and we then rest in the peace of true happiness. The falsehoods and cloudiness of not knowing whither away, and the light from our souls shines out from us in a glory that humbles us. The seesaw of our emotions and struggle release themselves and dissipate. There, behind the veil of our past misconceptions, stands the realization of the truth. We are free. We are empowered. We are the spark of our Father in physical form. Our light is lit from our Father's flame; it will never expire. We cannot die, because we are Him. We are eternal and a perfect being. All of our efforts to achieve any goal we desire can be accomplished. The world opens itself up to us, because it realizes itself in us. As we shine out our light, it reflects itself back to us. We are it, and it surrounds us. We stand in the presence of our True Self, which is our Father. No being or harm can destroy our soul. Being of good cheer, we endure the struggle; the reward is eternal happiness and peace within ourselves.

HOW DOES HONESTY BRING US TO TRUE HAPPINESS?

We feel ourselves letting go of the old ideas that have drained our energy by causing so much tension. Each turn we take seems more right, and each new day offers more opportunities. Life presents its stumbling blocks, traps, and mirrors of illusion to ensnare our soul in its web of mazes. However, the key resides in our honesty to ourselves. The truth that resides within us smooths out the terrain of our life, so we can walk with dignity, which is a reflection of our True Self. The clarity that arises from our increased awareness cuts the strings of self-doubt from our mind, and the pain of inadequacy from our heart. The never-ending flow of energy from our very being provides us a ride through life that fulfills our every desire. Then, as each moment turns into the next, we reach eternity, and in eternity, we bask in the sunlight of our Father's love and care. So we then turn our heart and mind to the truth of our very nature and stay focused on our goal of eternal love and salvation. We accept the challenges that lay before us; they are the road to our true happiness.

WHAT MUST WE DO TO TRULY BE WITH OUR FATHER?

It rears its head and comes after us, like an angry man with a two-by-four in his hands. Confrontation shakes our soul and brings us to our knees. Childhood memories flash before us and give rise within us to a great uneasiness that accompanies our tension. Our mind spins with scenarios of what to say and do, to no avail. The energy dispenses from us, as tiny arrows attack our body and diffuse it like the air that escapes from pricks on a balloon. Our greatest challenge lies before us.

To free ourselves from the fear and despair that grip us, we must stand up for ourselves. No compromise exists here. Our mind and heart must remain strong and evoke the respect we hold for ourselves and who we are. We can conquer the fears that reside within us, which have found a comfortable, cozy home for so many years. We can stick up for ourselves—we must—and, in doing so, we affirm the wholeness that resides within us. The only way our soul can be released to its freedom is if we take our stand and see ourselves as strong, confident, and brilliantly aware of the truth inside us. We deserve a life of freedom and happiness that knows no bounds and presents no limits. Through the grace of our Father and the confidence our True Self, we take a stand today. We plant our stake and declare who we are and that we can live in glory with our Father. His gift and His gift alone is who we are.

HOW DO WE LET ILL THOUGHTS GO?

Recurring thoughts run through our mind like a strong wind that never ceases. This same theme replays scenarios that arise from daily events we allow to cause us anxiety and anger. Now, as we begin to see ourselves ever more clearly, we gradually realize our godliness. Our self-assurance proclaims itself, and we begin to enjoy a newfound freedom. Just as small steps brought us through utter turmoil and the admittance of low self-esteem, we now proceed slowly to gather our rewards. Now, from the same daily events of ridicule and teasing by narrow minds, we reap the promise of better days. We raise ourselves up over the din of mediocrity by allowing ourselves to capture our very soul. For no one's words, intentions, or acts can diminish another's worth. Only we can do that to ourselves. So, let the world come, with its ignorance and meaningless chatter. As we see it for what it is, we dispel it from our mind. We see the truth of ourselves and embrace it by completely honoring ourselves and loving ourselves with our whole heart. We remain focused on our perfection. Only then will the patterns of thought that arise from the insecurities of anxiety and anger cease and wither away.

HOW DO WE BE OURSELVES?

It's all right to feel bad. In fact, we've done it a lot. We allow ourselves to feel the way we want to feel. Freedom lies in that. We march to our own drum and beat it loudly. We are who we are, and that cannot be changed, nor should we desire it to change. The right choice is to uncover ourselves and delve into the eternity and infinity of what lies there. It's our right to be ourselves. The rest is utter madness. The truth resides in fact that, if everyone honors themselves in totality and knows their True Self, all mankind would reside in peace. A misconception would cry selfishness. However, the ignorance of one's own soul gives rise to misconceptions and false beliefs. The dogma of religions and the search for achievements for their own sake leave a hollow emptiness that clanks like a ball bearing in an empty metal drum. Ignorance sets itself up as a combatant against wisdom. That displays foolishness and fruitlessness. In reality, ignorance does not exist. So, if it does not exist, there is nothing to fear. The only answer resides in unfolding our True Self and watching it manifest in the physical world. The more it manifests, the stronger its light, and the more assured and safer we feel. As we risk, we feel safer. We do not risk for risk's sake, but for our own sake. We discover the universe that lies within us. We let it blossom. It needs to grow. Its very nature dictates that life is for growing, and, through growth, we live.

WHERE DOES OUR FREEDOM LIE?

We feel our True Self well up inside us and make its way through the small crevices we have opened to let its light shine outward. The opportunities for expression present themselves to us, and we begin to embrace them. Ignorance and narrow-mindedness continually rear their ugly heads, and we still stand in amazement as closed minds spill out misconceptions onto the surface of life. Fear grips a closed mind and shuts it tightly, locking it and walking away with the key. Our own growth and awareness present the only way to deal with flat, "board-like" mentalities. Low self-esteem and self-confidence cling to us like a newborn baby to their mother's bosom. As we crack the egg of this learned limitation and begin to wipe away the mucus that has clung to our soul for so long, we begin to take our first steps of true freedom. Our movement is wobbly at best, but as we focus on the truth within, we slowly no longer see the dismal, self-imposed tragedy of low self-worth we dragged along for so many years. As our awareness grows, we allow ourselves expression; through expression, we realize and manifest our freedom. Yes, as we realize more, our freedom expands upon itself into a never-ending cycle of happiness.

WHAT BRINGS US FORWARD AND KEEPS US GOING?

We redeem ourselves from the soiled years of self-doubt caused by repression of emotions and expression. The fluidity of our soul always remains, because its essence is freedom. Although the journey appears long, it's a misconception. We have no cause to travel; we have arrived at our destination already. We have always been there. We strive to open our mind and heart to the truth that lies within us. We need not be disheartened that we still walk the path to freedom. We look at our progress and are happy, comforted, and confident. We apply our whole self to the solitary task of realizing our freedom. *It's ours. We have always had it.* We just forgot who we really are. We embrace the reality of our rightful place as we stand with our Father. We know that each man, woman, and child stands in equality, because we are and always have been free. We bind ourselves to our upbringing and play the same thoughts over and over during our earthly stay, but no more—we say no more. Each habit can be broken, and each negative thought will simply wither away. We will be left with our soul, and that's all we need. Discouragement is a fallacy. Courage is the horse we ride.

HOW DO WE PROGRESS THROUGH THESE DARK TUNNELS IN OUR MIND?

As we walk down the long, dark hallways, we begin to see a glimmer of light drawing us to it. It urges us to continue our way toward it. Although we sometimes stumble and fall in the darkness, we make our way slowly and assuredly, as our steps become lighter. Each passage presents itself, and we turn to face it and make our way through the obstacles it lays before us. Honesty guides us, and trust in ourselves propels us along the way. The next obstacle fearsomely looms at the end of the hallway, lying in wait. Its tentacles stretch out to intimidate us and stop us where we stand. However, we proceed with newfound vigor and confidence. We slay it, and it falls to the ground. This mighty dragon was nothing at all but a projection from our mind. And now it is gone. The only truth is us and our Father.

HOW DO WE EMPOWER OURSELVES?

We grapple less. We wonder 'why' less. Therefore, we stand more self-assured. Principles, dogmas, and beliefs established by society and its structures are not our own. They tie us down and keep us beholding to church, civic, financial, and even family powers. Life's most precious gift is the opportunity to discover our own power. We tie ourselves in knots, pleasing others and bowing to pressures that force us into a box of thinking that provides no room for freedom. Self-empowerment can only come through self-discovery. Through self-discovery, one grows; those that truly honor and love us allow our growth to occur. Those that feel threatened by the manifestation of our empowerment are manipulators of our destiny for their own good. So, as the discovery of ourselves expands, the questions become less, and the peace we share with our Father becomes more. That's all there is to it.

HOW IS HAPPINESS ACHIEVED?

The challenges lie before us and provide us opportunities to discover our True Self. Peace comes only through the work of letting go of old beliefs about ourselves and about how we thought the world works. The clarity that arises from dropping old misconceptions brightens our life and provides us more command of it. Fear and self-doubt are cripplers of happiness. They cause hesitancy and unfocused direction. So we continue on and are vigilant, and with this new awareness, we bypass old traps and discover new snares we were once unaware of. To wonder is to question. To know is to achieve. When we follow our heart, even though we might fall, we *are* happy. Happiness comes from trust in ourselves.

We must be aware, however, of the devil of arrogance. Arrogance leads us down a path of self-destruction. So, along our journey of growth, we must be honest with ourselves. We focus on our goal of happiness. We accept our failures as stepping stones to our peace. We become aware of self-fulfillment versus selfishness. We most of all bend our knee to our Father's every command. He only wants happiness for us.

WHAT IS THE WAY TO FINDING THE TRUTH ABOUT OURSELVES?

The trappings of old, worn-out thoughts will not leave until we tell them to go. Just as persistent as they are to stay, we must be persistent that they depart our mind forever. The ball and chain of thoughts of inadequacy and non-self-recognition must be broken. They shade our achievements, cover our self-worth, and impair us from seeing our True Self. Our talents abound, and our mind enjoys its opportunities to let the creativity flow unhampered. Our yearning to totally allow ourselves freedom is just that. We must decide to risk failure in order to gain success. We must decide to truly honor who we are and dismiss the detrimental remarks of others. We must decide that our life is our life, and only we know how to truly lead it. Fear hangs on, and its lingering intrudes on our true potential. We must cast off our doubts and completely trust our instincts. If we fall, we must get up. If they laugh, we must continue. If they try to trip us and make us fall, we must walk over their snares. We must continue, no matter the cost; the rewards are great. No one can put us down but ourselves. We must drop the old ways and renew ourselves through our own realizations.

HOW DO WE GAIN SELF-LOVE?

Our life truly reflects back to us the accumulation of all our thoughts and emotions. As we peel off the layers of suppressed emotions, we now see more clearly the truth of our past years on our road to this point. With pride, we now allow ourselves to acknowledge all our successes with the same honesty, truth, and sincerity we have bestowed upon others. Even with the sack of stones we have carried on our back, our journey has brought us far. At times, on the path of life, we have even crawled.

Now, we begin to raise ourselves up, as we ease our load and start to enjoy our walk. We begin to take on a different perspective from this new vista of our life. We no longer need to chastise ourselves or be impatient with our progress. Instead, we recognize our achievements over subtleties imposed upon us in our early years, which had trapped us in an emotional box tied with a web to ensnare us and keep us from escaping. We see ourselves more clearly. Our intellect carries a sharp sword to cut through problems. Our heart provides compassion and empathy as it rises from its wounds. Our humor brings a tender touch and lightens our load. We stop our own chastisements and begin to see who we are as well as all of our achievements, regardless of the emotional handicap we carried for ourselves and others. We are good enough. We are progressing. We assure ourselves the successful goal of happiness. This is our plan. This is our destiny.

HOW DO WE BREAK THE BINDINGS OF THE PAST?

The sweetness of life awaits those who march to its doorstep. Each man carries his cross, but at his journey's end, he lays it down and walks away. From the pedestal of happiness, he sees that the burdens he has carried molded his strength and forged his courage to see beyond all limitations. We alone hold ourselves back, and in doing so, we wander the desert of life, walking in circles. However, as we focus on the goal of happiness and move forward with resolve and determination, the world supports our efforts. Opportunities for growth present themselves, and we allow ourselves to earn our way up to the mountaintop. The search for awareness reciprocates with the illumination of our mind and the presentation of clarity. The path opens up; the way is certain. Then we must gather up ourselves and press on to the gates of heaven, where our Father awaits us with unending love.

HOW DO WE REACH OUR SUCCESS?

We can and must succeed. With our last breath, we vow our victory to ourselves and to our Father. Courageously, we proceed, but only through humility can we let loose the trumpets of angels as their song is heard throughout heaven. Our soul aches to be saved from the earthly bowels of ignorance, injustice, and ridicule of righteousness. There is no easy task, but we accept our fate. Through our own will and our Father's grace, we carry our sword of courage. The treachery that lies before us planted its seeds a long time ago. The vines of entanglement possess deep roots and boast strength to never falter and die. Still, we must seek out these demons deep inside our mind, face them, and pull them out one by one. We see the light through this thicket before our eyes. Its warmth beckons us to come in from the cold and darkness that has encompassed our life. Our time for victory is now, and we claim it. The righteousness of our Father fills us and with patience, firmness, and love. We allow our freedom to gently land in our lap, where we cherish it forever.

WHAT DECISION MUST WE MAKE?

Our spirit refreshed itself today, as we caught a glimpse of the way home. The power of free will flashed its light on us and showed us the way to our True Self. In the scheme of life, all past events, thoughts, and emotions bring us to this current moment; only in the current moment can we change ourselves. No teacher, group, wife, husband, or loved one can transform our mind to see the light within ourselves. Only we can decide to throw off the barnacles of our past life and accept ourselves without condition. The pure love of ourselves frees us to express ourselves with unbridled creativity. We must love our Father with our whole heart, mind, and strength. When we pass through this "eye of the needle," we will be home. Only we alone can make this decision to love the glory and the godliness of ourselves.

WHAT IS FREEDOM?

Freedom only comes when we accept it. We wander around for years, looking for it, while it waits patiently for us to see it and welcome it into our minds and hearts. Free will is the lever we push when we go from turmoil and wanting to a peaceful existence that no words can possibly describe. Complete surrender holds the answer. We must surrender to the godliness within ourselves; from that springs everlasting life.

That is the covenant of our Father to all His children. If we see Him, honor Him, and love Him with all our might, He will lavish us with the gift of Himself as we walk with the dignity and grace of Him. We don't need to own anything anymore. We simply use the material belongings our Father has given us. We don't need to strive and struggle to earn more money, fame, or stature. That makes no sense. If we are free to roam the earth and have all our needs met anywhere and anytime, we want for nothing. There is no need to struggle. Complete contentment with ourselves offers this freedom to us. We can achieve anything, or we can put our feet up and watch the clouds all day—it does not matter. To know we are always taken care of by our Father provides a peace and freedom no king can possibly possess. We must drop all our attachments to physical things, emotional longings, and obsessive thoughts. When we decide to accept and love ourselves, we do not desire or need anything else. That is freedom.

HOW DO WE MOVE INTO THE LIGHT?

We let ourselves relax and enter our new life. We simply walk forward and meet it with the grace we have earned from our journey. We feel certainty fill us from our past successes. We walk from the darkness into the light and are naturally at home and calm. We wake up and smile, because we know the journey we set out on prepared us for the rewards we now reap. Heaven opens its gates to us, because we honor ourselves. Our Father smiles, because He knows we love Him. Our days began to fill themselves with activities of fulfillment. Small flowers of joy begin to sprout, and a soft rain falls to nourish their growth. As we stay in the moment, we shed the past. As we stay in the moment, we meet the future. The flow of life rushes to greet us, and we feel less struggle. Our mind becomes illumined and our sight becomes clear. As we trust ourselves, our intuition becomes stronger and our way becomes easier, because we know where we are going. We control our world and command our destiny. We engage and accept who we really are. We accept our victories and allow ourselves the right to walk free. As our Father's children, we are entitled to His love and His gift of peace, which we now accept.

HOW DO WE REALIZE THE I AM WITHIN US?

The Light shines through the window of our soul. Deep within us lies the truth we seek, and it will not be denied itself. As we grasp the realities of life, it sets us free to be ourselves. As we realize and accept our own talents, it gives us pause. Right here, in our own midst, lies the end to our journey. As we begin to explore our newfound freedom, calm and peace come over us that we never knew before. We deserve these abundant rewards, simply because we are our Father's child. He loves us; from His bounty, we are the I Am. We realize our true existence and walk on the earth, lighter in Spirit. Our way is made clear, and we walk with poise and dignity. Trials come; let them. They only represent opportunities for us to open our mind more to the grace within ourselves. Yes, the time has come for us, to see our True Self; then, we can rest. Then, we can let our life flow. The struggle will be over. We can live free.

HOW DOES SELF-REALIZATION FREE US FROM OUR FEARS?

The peace of our soul settles into our mind and body. This precious gift manifests itself in our life. With a new awareness, we pull back layers of illusions that once clouded our judgment and spoiled our days. Life's harpoons of ignorance, injustice, and selfishness take their aim, but now we enter into a new dimension of our real Self. The simplicity of self-realization frees the illusions of our fears, so we are more able to handle life's cruelties. Our beginning efforts resemble a child as he takes his first steps. However, the determination that brought us to this point will carry us into a full stride that will last forever. Our heritage awaits us. The promise of pure happiness and unending freedom turns into more of a reality day by day.

HOW DO WE MAKE OUR WAY ALONG THE PATH WE TAKE?

The pain remains, because we are allowing it to stay. As we decide to release our pain, the world looks differently to us. The same ruts in our mind remain, but their depth grow more shallow. As we fill our life with the truth of ourselves, the road becomes more smooth. We hold our head higher. Our heart feels lighter, and our mind relaxes into its newfound clarity. We do not stand still on our journey, but proceed step by step. Although our progress appears slow, in reality it is not; in reality, no time exists. The challenges we face must be conquered. Although we appear clumsy in our early attempts, we do make our way forward. Belief in ourselves shows the way to our freedom. As we realize the light within ourselves, we see the challenges as illusions. These illusions fade away, because the mind no longer holds them as real. Our Father does not forsake us. We are rich with His Spirit. So, now, we must delve even deeper to pull out the old roots that have clouded our mind. We ask our Father to speak to us and give us the strength to follow Him.

HOW IS LIFE MASTERED?

The indignities of life wait for those that allow them to happen. Choices made long ago see their results occur now. Life hands out its hardships, and those who fail to meet them head-on become crushed by their blow or ensnared in their thorny nets. Peace comes only through courage. Courage springs from a soul that realizes itself. Arrogance and stupidity force one to smash into the wall of the hardships of life. Timidity and fear entrap the soul into a hell of self-doubt and self-pity. Acceptance of one's fate and resolution to overcome the barriers and hurdles of life evoke a resilience of the soul that knows no bounds. So we must be firm in our commitment and flexible with our methods of achievement. In that way, we reap our rewards. Life lies there for the taking; we are its master.

HOW DO WE ENTER INTO OUR NEW LIFE?

Our life lights up with a sparkle that illumines from our soul. Our vision becomes more focused and clear. The way is made easier for us. We now taste the fruit from the seeds we planted. Each branch of our life sprouts more fully; we have pulled the weeds from our mind to allow its growth. Now, we let our new life take shape and reveal its mysteries to us. Simplicity is the answer, and it can only be realized through complete surrender. Total trust in ourselves is the key to unlocking the doors of our life that once were shut and seemed impenetrable. Now, these doors swing open wide to reveal a light that beckons us to come out and enjoy its radiance and warmth. The surprises of our life await us as we grow to meet them.

In our heart, we know this truth. We set out on a new direction and walk naturally to our destiny. Our Father waits for us there. He has urged us along the way to come to Him. As we lift this sack of ignorance from around our head, we envision an inkling of our new life. We let reality transform our mind, and we accept it. It is the only way to our freedom. Let us not make freedom our goal; dear Father, let us simply accept the gift of freedom that has been bestowed upon us. We ask for the strength to truly honor You by honoring ourselves. Help us to know You, beloved Father.

HOW IS OUR WAY MADE CLEAR?

The shadowy corners of our life expose themselves to us. What once was hidden in darkness, we can now see and sweep away. Peace fills us as we make this transition in our life. We understand more, which settles us down and provides us a new degree of self-assurance. Our progress comes to us at the pace we allow. Our intellect grasps the concepts, but our soul lives them. No words can describe our rewards, and no one can take them from us. We look out at our life, which offers us promise and fulfillment. Our tender heart and sensitive nature we once saw as weaknesses are really our greatest strengths. They allow us the insight into the realities of the world, and therefore free us from the world's grasp. Freedom tips its hat to us, and we nod back with a smile. Our face shines in the dawn of a new life that can only get better.

HOW DO WE LIVE IN EACH MOMENT?

We engage each moment with the focus and attention of someone that walks on a high wire beam. Unless we do this, life slips away. The moments turn into hours, the hours into days, and the days into years. Before we know it, our life has passed us by. It does not wait for us. So we must affirm to ourselves our resolve to throw away "should have's" from the past and "when we have's" from the future. The gift of life stands ready and waiting for us right now. It reaches out its hand to us. We take it and enjoy its surprises, learning from its trials and sometimes squirting water out of our nose, just for the fun of it. We teach ourselves to release the tension caused by our desire to keep everything in order. When we drop this impossible task, we begin to live. We honor ourselves and let the world just be. As we walk in our own light, life opens its doors to us, and we live in each moment.

WHAT DO WE NEED TO DO TO TRUST LIFE?

We need to stop pushing, and instead let it come and land in our hand like an elusive butterfly. We allow the day to present itself to us and enjoy its surprises and unfoldments. We watch the drama of life and take the time to laugh at ourselves. Life belongs to us and we belong to it. Our heartbeat and our very breath reflect the ebb and flow of life. As we make our own way, life runs to support us. We follow those tiny inklings that softly nudge us, and then watch as the world unfolds before us. We are courageous and stay on the course as our instincts guide us. We walk with our heads high and stay present. That is where our answers lie. We know what to do, and we know how to do it. We trust ourselves and laugh at ourselves when we lock our keys in our car. Lessons bring us into the present moment and make us focus. Life is for those who allow it to run freely. It will anyway. To try and control events is futile. We give up and let happiness land in our lap.

HOW IS CONSCIOUSNESS GAINED?

Slowly, the curtain falls from in front of our eyes. The knots that kept it in place begin to loosen, and it goes limp. Its tattered fabric exposes the light through its flimsiness. Realizations come, and we have nothing to do but let the curtain fray and fall. Nothing can be permanent that is not real. This curtain was only a figment of our mind that weaved its pattern with density over so many years. This caused darkness and doubts. Now, the curtain hangs without support, and begins its descent as it withers away into nonexistence. With eyes wide open and our mind alert, we allow life to fill us with its grace and wonders. We let it touch our brow softly. We hear its rhythm. We taste its joy and smell the sweetness of its rose. We see it for the first time and enjoy its offerings.

HOW DO WE REALIZE THE FLOW OF LIFE?

Slowly, ever so slowly, the sun rises and the dawn of a new day begins. The glimmer of new light then turns into a brightness that shines upon the world so it can see itself. Naturally, we move slowly into the dawn of our life as the darkness of our ignorance surrenders to the promise of our True Self. Insight springs from inside us and illumines our mind. Understanding helps us drop attachments and settles us into our natural state. Life comes as we let it; the more we push, the more life conceals itself from us. The more we trust in ourselves and allow the outcomes, the swifter we float down the river of life. We enjoy its twists and turns and beauty. We laugh with excitement when we spill over into a new waterfall. Our hand has reached the rudder of our life. Now, we steer our own course. Flow, river, flow.

WHAT DOES SPIRIT GIVE US?

Our Spirit rises up from within us and reveals itself. We are aware of its presence, and with that realization, we engage life. The peace that fills us defies words. We see life with all its beauty as well is its deceit and manipulation. Guided by a freer heart and with the instrument of a clearer mind, we make our way more easily through life. We do not need a cloak of armor or a weapon of mighty force to protect ourselves. Indeed, as we see a clear picture, no need exists for us to defend ourselves. As we grow, we see we cannot truly depict anyone as an enemy, nor can they single us out for destruction. This concept is a fallacy. When the Spirit knows itself, it knows it cannot be destroyed. Awareness brings understanding. Understanding brings peace. Peace brings happiness, and happiness lives in eternity. This earth plane is not finality, but instead is an opportunity for us to use its lessons to see the eternal. Spirit rests in eternity.

HOW IS OUR WAY MADE CLEAR?

At long last, this narrow, rocky road we travel starts to widen, and our way becomes more smooth. Our Father's promises become realities, and the signposts to freedom reveal themselves to us. Emotions still cloud the way, but they begin to lose their power. To take command of ourselves is the ultimate reward to a fulfilling life. As we reveal our own weaknesses and face them, we become stronger. The turmoil from our past hangs on for its very life. Slowly, very slowly, it loses its hold.

We alone must release these negative emotions that have tied us down to a life of wandering in a circle of uncertainty and fear. Our happiness waits patiently for us. We want to know it. We want to heal our wounds and stand straight and tall. We want to feel our own strength. We want to be our own person. We want to enjoy our life and see it flourish and grow. So we must continue on and dispel the devils that linger. We must be patient and loving with ourselves; untying these emotional knots is no easy task. With faith in ourselves and the help of our very dear family and friends, we can triumph. Nothing can stand in our way. We are assured of our happiness.

WHAT ARE OUR TRUE REWARDS?

We must be patient and take time with ourselves. Our bounty has always been there for us. With confidence, we can accept it now. With love for our Father, we give thanks. The feelings from the past fade away; with their disappearance, the glory of our Father presents itself. The Kingdom of our Father truly lies within us; no need exists to chase it down or achieve it as a prize. We raise ourselves up to meet our True Self. We let the voice from within us guide our way. We are assured of our True Self and continue in confidence. Our past victories have paved our way. Our heart feels the gentleness of our soul. Our mind lights up with clarity and vision. Our courage carries us forward. We see our progress and know it is real.

Now, our energy begins to build force and opens us to a full life, with riches even the greatest earthly king does not have. So we continue to be alert and observe ourselves. We see the play of the world unfold and take our rightful place in it. We spread the goodness of our soul outward with the energy that is ours to give. We use our talents wisely. We take time to watch the clouds pass by and listen to the birds sing early in the morning. What once was doubt and fear disappear, and we can now rest in ourselves and enjoy the peace we know has always lived there.

WHAT BRINGS US OUT OF THE WORLD'S GRIP?

The merry-go-round of life keeps spinning faster and faster at a fero-cious pace. However, we see it now. Our thoughts become slower and more powerful. We are more focused and act with more preci-sion within the hecticness of life. We bear more fruit and enjoy life with less effort. Our observations bring insight, which in turn provides us understanding. Understanding dissipates the anger, because the anger has no room to exist. Life smooths out and welcomes us with its true reality instead of its mirrors of deception. As we see with more clarity, we don't trip and fall; instead, we walk confidently to the destinations of our choice. By funneling the energy our Father provides us through our talents, we reap rewards no words can begin to describe. Our free will provides the lever for good or evil, achievement or suffering, happiness or despair. Our mind discerns the path, and determination carries us through to the fruition of our own choices. Whether we want to admit it or not, the realities we see in our own lives are of our own making. We take comfort in that, rather than in dread or regret. We do command ourselves, whether down the path of righteousness to heaven or through misconceptions that enslave us in a hell we probably don't know we are even in. We listen to ourselves and see the Spirit of our Father that lies within us. We walk in its rhythm.

HOW DO WE BREAK FREE FROM WHAT BINDS US?

The devils keep lurching inside us, hiding and disguising themselves. However, we begin to realize their days dwindle as we allow the light to stream from our soul. As our awareness expands, it banishes despair and leaves in its place only triumph. To each stumbling block we cross, each snare we untangle, each heartache we let go of, we say goodbye and farewell. The breath of life becomes easier, and we become stronger and move more effortlessly. Awareness stops the suffering, which vanishes; it is not reality. Life continues on, and as we accept it, it flows more easily. No longer do we need to be entangled in its web of sadness and deceit.

The joys of freedom must be earned. Awareness can only come from dropping old conditioning, old beliefs, and all the harmful emotions attached to very old experiences. Patterns in life replay themselves from past experiences. This earthly journey allows us to break the cycle of dependency, despair, doubt, and fear. The world displays its wares of ridicule, stupidity, and carelessness. Now, we have the choice to allow them to affect us or know that we are beautiful, eternal, loving human beings.

WHAT IS TRUE LOVE FOR OURSELVES AND OTHERS?

The conflicts arise, but we need to stand our ground. We must remain poised and honor ourselves. To please others does not make them happy, nor does it make us happy. It is contrived, and sets up a situation of dependency. They feel better, because they are in control; we feel better, because they like us. This situation is a farce, and provides no lasting support or sustenance for anyone. Our lives have contained years of servitude to our family's and friends' wants and desires, to fill their lives from the emptiness they have felt deep in their hearts. It is better for us and them to break this cycle of dominance and submissiveness, and instead set up a pattern of equality and true love.

No person should desire, consciously or unconsciously, to dominate another. No person should feel ill enough of themselves to submit their freedom to another. Each of us remains free, in reality. If we lose sight of reality, we wander around aimlessly and wonder why we are not content and happy. Life offers us trials in small and great proportions. We must use them to shape our characters. Let us stand up and be free. Let us treat each other equally. Let us respect and care for each other. Let us grow and support the growth of our loved ones and friends. Our thought patterns bring us down roads of detriment and despair or to the richness of happiness. Let us be honest with ourselves and those we deal with. That is where true love lies.

WHAT DOES BEING TRUE TO OURSELVES BRING?

Our lives have sung a very sad song for many years. We cried out in fear and then anger. Our realizations now expose the truth of our upbringing. Life is life, and we need to face it. In doing so, we not only free ourselves, we free those that are dear to us. Our Father's light can only shine on the truth. When we are not true to ourselves, our Father cannot be there. We need to open the door for Him to come in and shine His Light through us. When we despair or fear, the flow of life cannot pour out from our souls. By being true to ourselves, we feel the calmness that is truly ours. Then we allow our love to pour out to those around us. Those that never cared about us will leave or crawl back into their holes of deceit. Those who truly love us will be enriched by our honesty, and a further binding of our love with them will occur. Love begets love, and it becomes stronger as we become more honest with ourselves and those around us.

HOW DO WE CLAIM OUR RIGHT AS OUR FATHER'S CHILDREN?

The mind races incessantly about matters that never happened or never will happen. Our plights dress themselves up with fantasies that only cause undue tension, anxiety, and fruitlessness. Our pent-up emotions contribute to undue suffering. As we realize the old patterns that have shaped our life, we see the opportunity to drop them from our very existence and therefore walk free. Anger proudly takes on the role of the spoiler. Its intensity becomes strong as the ego eggs it on. Anger cries out and says "I can't." But the ego's days are numbered; its life of dominance wanes as it falters and weakens to its very death. Life is truly for the living. The peace of our soul provides the strength to step out in boldness and proclaim the love that resides in our heart. Let the madness end and the truth be seen. All of us are our Father's children. We simply need to claim our right to the gift of our Father Himself.

HOW IS LOVE UPHELD IN OUR RELATIONSHIPS?

Our lives resound with the scattering of misgivings that occurred through a lack of awareness. To claim our soul at this stage of our life demands the price of great uncomfortableness. Behavior accrued in this temporal existence turns into patterns not easily shaken, let alone dissolved. However, determination provides the wings to freedom. If we free ourselves, we free those with whom we hold relationships. The love of a devoted spouse and the loyalty of true friends will weather the tumultuous journey of our relationship as we step toward freedom. The ego, as usual, lies in waiting to derail our efforts, but vigilance sees the game and ensures a smoother path. So let the silence come, and be in it. If the unraveling of dependent behavior causes anxiety and friction as it falls apart, let it. True love, devotion, and loyalty bring rewards of true happiness, not only to the individual but also to our true friends.

WHERE DOES VIRTUE LIVE?

Deep inside us lies the virtue we seek. As we peel away the layers of time and the patterns of servitude, an awareness rises up from us that eases our path. Temptations rise along the way that try to derail our growth or try to discourage us into retreating into the old ways. Disappointments mount up along the way, but as growth occurs, our sicknesses become less severe and less frequent. The past is gone; it cannot be retrieved and lived again, and it should not be. Facing life as it comes is the true test of character, and the lessons learned bring successes. However, the awareness gained opens up a wider path that brings us an opportunity for the enjoyment of life. The sharp edges are rounded out, the grind gets eased, and life's beauty begins to reveal itself. We must be true to ourselves and feel the newness of this experience. It frees us and makes us whole. We need not be rigid, but simply flow with the promptings that come to us.

HOW DOES OUR FAITH SERVE US?

As we are of good faith, it will light our way to any achievement. Whether our goal is healing, wisdom, or prosperity, the candle we must hold in our heart and mind must be faith. It lights the fire of our determination and allows us to focus on the tasks at hand. Faith gives us comfort in our darkest hours. Be ye of great faith, and accomplish great things. Be ye of little faith, and live in a life of squalor and contempt. Our good Father allowed us this great faculty to bring us along our way and finally back to Him. So let us rise in the morning to good cheer. In the evening, let us lay our heads down on our pillow in the comfort of knowing our journey is assured of success. Let us enjoy the fruits of our labor that are made possible by the faith we have in ourselves and in our Father, who put it there.

HOW DO WE SHINE OUR UNIQUENESS?

We all possess the majesty of our own individualities. That spark of uniqueness that lies in all of us carries with it great potential. It is up to each of us, however, to fan that flame and light a burning passion that never goes out. The beauty of this mosaic called the human race lies simply in the fact that no one rises above another. No one carries more gifts than another. The gifts are just different. The choices each individual makes to allow their gifts to grow reflects how far one's light will shine out into the world. Fame, fortune, and recognition create false measures. Uncovering talents and nurturing them brings happiness to the individual and all those they touch. As we release the burdens from the past, our energy rises. As our energy rises, we see our gifts. As we see our gifts, we use them. As we use them, we become more happy. As we become more happy, we bless the world with our love. This is truth.

WHAT IS THE PATH TO MASTERING OUR LIFE?

We must release the tension from our mind and put our trust in the process of life. As we steer our boat through troubled waters, our awareness rises, our senses become more keen, and we build more confidence. As tragedies befall us, we face them and carry our head high. We refuse to let them drag us into despair. We ride these rough waves, avoid the jagged rocks, and then move smoothly into calm waters. Life continually presents its currents to us. We flow with them. As we learn how to master them, we surely become the captain of our own ship.

WHAT DOES THE TRUTH REVEAL TO US?

Our spirit urges us to continue along our path, which offers us many opportunities to expand the awareness of our Father. The true realities exist within our heart and mind. They wait, ready to be discovered by us. Our fear stands in the way and intrudes on the very happiness we seek and will find. As we see the truth, it releases us of burdens we have carried for such a long time. Truth opens our lives up to promise and joy. It sets our world into order. Freedom beckons us to its arms.

As we become stronger from our trials and triumphs, we build a courage that will take us to a higher place. As we see the light of truth and the glory it dispenses, we reap the peace that pours out over us. Life offers itself to us as a gift to reach the ultimate of ourselves realized. Each stepping stone of fear conquered peels away the dismal trappings of an old life that hangs on for its very existence. May we know ourselves, and revel in the glory of our Father's house. May we honor Him when we honor ourselves. May we know Him and bask in the joy He bestows upon us. May we kneel at His feet and pray for the touch of His hand upon our head. May we see the truth that is ourselves.

WHAT IS OUR HERITAGE?

The spirit of truth rises up in us and calms us to our very soul. Our heart beats gently, with the rhythm of a child. Our body relaxes to its natural state, and the tension withers away. Our affairs come into order, and our life displays the harmony it was always meant to. As the butterflies flutter from flower to flower for their nourishment, our mind dances with quiet thoughts that string themselves together with a silk thread of belief and everlasting life. This is our heritage, and it brings with it our entitlement to happiness. Our Father granted us the power to achieve anything our heart desires. As we follow the urgings of our heart, a drab existence gives way to a beauty beyond all beauty. Our soul, freed from the ravages of imprisonment, reaches to the stars and beyond. Its life emanates from our very being, and shines forever with the love of our Father, who keeps its eternal flame burning within us.

WHAT DOES IT MEAN TO BE ALIVE?

The brittle façade of our past existence dries up from lack of nourishment. The doubts and fears that once fed on its hearty meals of self-pity and lack of self-worth come no more. The cracks that started its decay now assist in its destruction, as pieces of old crust fall and break apart like an old vase that slips to the floor. Its death signifies a new beginning of self-assuredness, confidence, laughter, and a peace that knows no bounds. So we say: begone, darkness and despair. Crawl back into your nonexistence, and disappear into the nothingness you are. In our new life, our Father's love sustains us, His grace uplifts us, and His joy lavishes upon us a happiness that brings with it an eternity of peace. We thank our Father we are alive.

WHAT IS ETERNAL LIFE?

We enjoy the grace of our Father and walk with the confidence of an angel who lives in the eternity of His arms. The precious gift of life lays out itself to smooth our rough edges by placing obstacles and traps along our way. The obstacles we overcome make us stronger. The traps we realize and then avoid make us wiser. We climb out of the dark hole of ignorance that kept us covered in its shame. Now we walk in the world, ready to meet it. Along this journey, we depend on our own determination and the truth that lies within us. The riches we uncover from within ourselves illumine our mind and expose our many strengths and weaknesses. Life continues on its way, and it is up to us how we meet it. Our choice remains to carry on, be courageous, never give in, and know that the victory of eternal life lies within ourselves.

HOW DO WE KNOW OURSELVES?

The trappings of our past life linger on, because we let them. Their stubbornness persists, in an effort to derail our progress and impede our destiny. However, nothing possesses power over us. Our life is our own to do with what we will. Our own self-image projects out to the world, and the world reacts to us. Our choice to really see ourselves releases us to show our true face to the world. We no longer hide behind dismal feelings, or any kind of inadequacy. We no longer feel not good enough. We no longer feel any endeavor we undertake will end in failure. Our God-given intelligence and desire to know our True Self unleash the power of our soul to overcome all past transgressions we inflicted upon ourselves or allowed others to impose upon us. Our mission is to see our Father's light and bask in its presence. Our duty is to unbind the harness of ignorance from our mind and walk freely in the knowledge of the goodness of ourselves. No person or circumstance can shake our house. We stand firm and strong. We bend only to the circumstances of life in the course of survival, not submission. We realize the true nature of ourselves. We know happiness and self-love. We know who we are—an eternal, vibrant, and loving human being.

WHERE DO OPPORTUNITIES LIE?

The road to a light heart comes through great patience, unending perseverance, and absolute faith in ourselves. Realizations may come in spurts, or through a long, enduring process. The way to freedom provides opportunity after opportunity with our continual commitment to unfolding the real us. We leave the mechanics of life to the sleepwalkers with dreams of grandeur. By casting off our negativity, life opens its arms with delight to embrace us and nurture our every desire. No free ride exists. Instead, life presents opportunities to grow in Spirit. Realities become more clear each day, and the glory of our very soul unfolds itself to us. We must be aware! We open our eyes, but we listen with our heart. Then, the world kneels at our doorstep.

WHERE IS THE LIGHT?

Refreshing raindrops of joy gently pitter-patter upon our life. The days grow less tedious and the struggle gradually decreases, as we gain control of our mind. As life displays its surprises, we accept them more gracefully, as the profound realization of ourselves comes to bear. Risks abound on this inward journey, but rewards of the victory of peace urge a determination to continue to unfold the powerful presence that lies within us. Truth bears witness in our search for it. Love provides the strength to traverse rocky roads. Our Father provides the answers, when asked. Faith ensures the right manifestations occur in our life, even though appearances might be deceptive. So, as we enjoy this new beauty, we must be vigilant not to overstep our bounds. This would spell disaster. Instead, we vow to let life unfold itself to us from within our very depths and watch it rise and display the light that emanates from our very soul.

WHAT IS INVINCIBILITY?

Our Father's guiding light reaches out to us to reveal our way. The steps are our own, but the path laid out truly brings us to everlasting happiness. Thought by thought, we turn over to a new life, filled with the riches of harmony and peace. Our awareness expands, and life opens its doors to its mysteries and then reveals its secrets to us. Simplicity of heart, clarity of mind, good intentions, and never-ending perseverance allow our True Self to be revealed to us. Willingness provides the spark. Determination lights the flame, and perseverance keeps it burning. Vigilance ensures the chills of the world will never overpower the warmth of our soul. Truly, truly, we are the fabric of our Father. wWe stand invincible, because we are Him.

HOW DO WE REALIZE LOVE?

Our inward journey unlocks the door to our deepest secrets. As we face our fears, our outward life takes on a new dimension. The clarity of our insights affords us an easier way. Our strength builds upon itself. Our happiness settles in. From this higher perspective, we are no longer victim but victor. Nay, our head cannot lie down in laziness. Rather, as we remain alert and follow the inklings of our soul, the world continues to open up to us. The game of life sings a sweeter song. The world will always display its wares of cruelty and deception, but our greater awareness shines its light into the dark corners that once frightened us. Step by step, we move forward with more confidence and love. As the fear dissipates, love remains; that is the only thing that is real anyway.

WHAT PATH MUST WE FOLLOW?

The great joy of eternal love warms us, as it shines from our soul. Its beauty fills us, as we drop the burdens from our heart. The stormy seas of our mind quiet, and a calm settles in that cannot be expressed in words. Realizations arise, as soft petals of awareness dance before our eyes and land gently at our feet. Our footsteps find their way forward down a path that reveals the essence of life itself. Gifts abound and stand ready. We allow them now to come, and we give great thanks for their blessings to us. Truly, we are rich when we walk the path of our Father. Our Savior lit the way, and we must follow Him. He truly is our salvation.

HOW DO WE TRAVERSE OUR PATH TO FREEDOM?

Our Father's gracious gift of life emboldens us to grasp it and use it wisely. Our intuition nods its head, and we follow. Our spirit tells the truth, and we heed its answer. Good books tell the story of truth, and great spiritual men speak from their hearts of the nature of our Father. However, we must use our own senses to taste of Him and smell the fragrance of His love. Only we alone can surrender to our True Self. Only we alone can hear our small voice whisper its truth to us. Only we alone can face the fears that haunt our soul and attempt to hide our true essence from ourselves. Our journey is ours alone, and we must take each step under our own power. Our earthly teachers guide us along our way. Our spouse comforts us and provides a peaceful home. However, we alone must reach deep into our soul and allow our True Self to take control of our life. This is our quest. This is our life. We now declare and dedicate ourselves to our freedom.

WHAT MUST WE DO TO GAIN OUR FREEDOM?

We embrace the passion within ourselves. We follow the urgings of our soul and feel alive. Life offers its abundance, when we free ourselves from the drudgery of others' problems. Creativity can only express itself when it is not weighed down or hampered by ignorance. Shortsightedness and narrow-mindedness fragment creativity, as they proceed to slice it up so it cannot raise its energy. People's agendas and motives pull at creativity to disaffirm or steal it for their own purpose. A free man who has earned his self-worth possesses energy that rises above fragmentation and manipulation. His insight leads him, and his awareness keeps him out of harm's way. We must be willing to be free. We need determination to gain freedom and vigilance to keep it. As we remember these things, life grants us abundant blessings.

HOW DO WE RELEASE OUR SOUL TO FREEDOM?

We grant ourselves the right to know our True Self. We free ourselves from the burdens we carry in our hearts. We drop the repetitive refuse that runs through our mind. We stand up to our fears and watch them fade into nothingness. We deserve to know ourselves. We take the road to freedom, and do not waver along the way. Our steadfastness grants us rewards of untold happiness. The subtleties of our life bring us the greatest joys. No words can describe our newfound freedom. The once rough edges of our life smooth out. The flow of our day gives rise to an observation of ourselves, playing out our part on the stage of life. Gradually, oh so gradually, our awareness expands and releases our soul to truly know its own glory. No stations in life exist. No pomp and ceremony are necessary. No money can buy happiness and freedom. Only by dropping the ravages from our mind can we free our heart and release our soul.

WHAT IS THE GREATEST GIFT?

Insights come as we allow them. Stagnation can remain for years, but willingness opens the door to the enlightenment of our heart. We wash the windows of our mind and let the light of our soul shine out. The beauty of who we are cannot be denied itself. The love of our Father filters through our individuality with the intensity of the measure of our awareness. The world challenges us with its negativity. As we overcome these misconceptions, we realize the true nature of ourselves. We uncover our talents and allow them to grow and flourish. We enrich ourselves and, by doing so, we pour out our light upon others. We need not be afraid; no one can deny us our right to freedom. Only we alone can do that. We claim our soul. We embrace our heritage. We let our heart sing with the joy of the essence of ourselves. We are eternal, vibrant, and true love. This is our Father's gift, that we are Him.

HOW DOES THE TRUTH REVEAL ITSELF TO US?

Blessings abide in our life as our awareness expands to light our way. We no longer stumble and fall, but instead see the rocks that tripped us and snares that entangled our mind. The heavens open up to us and show us their glory. The once fears and frustrations of our life dissolve, and true realities appear. Our perceptions, made more clear, give us the strength to address our shortcomings. Our will remains the rudder, and our determination the force to traverse our life. The world presents its negativity; that will not go away. However, by our awareness, we now walk free, and through our effort, our road smooths out and opens wide. So, day by day and moment by moment, our truth comes to us. It whispers in our ear and dances before our eyes. It beckons us to see more of it and more of ourselves.

HOW DOES LIFE CLEANSE US?

As we wake up from our slumber, we feel the vibrance of our soul. The realities of our life stand before us, and their goodness comforts us. The riches we seek cannot be bought, only earned. Every day brings opportunities for growth and realizations of truth. Special moments exist as we let them. Life lays out a platter of delectable treats of humor, honor, friendship, devotion, and love. To honestly partake of these gifts, we drop the veil of fear and walk to meet them. Our heart rests in contentment. Our mind rests in peace. Our very soul sees itself. The journey of truth beckons us, and we hear its soft whisper. We let it come in, and in its depths, we wash ourselves clean and see ourselves.

HOW DO WE SEE THE LIGHT?

We behold the glory of ourselves. From darkness to a dim light that peaks out from our real selves shines the truth of our souls. We hold to that light for it is our salvation. Darkness hangs on with its sordid tentacles, but to no avail. Eternity is on our side. With our willingness, we pick up the scrub brush of life's lessons and use them to wash away the darkness that seemingly surrounds our mind. Everyday negativity provides the opportunity for us to see it is a great mirage, a scheme to cover the true realities that lie within us. Holy, holy, holy are we. Our sanctity signifies our very essence. We drop the falsehoods of bad habits, corroded thinking, and any ideas of false beliefs. We face the fears that stand before us and watch them wither away at our feet. We meet our darkest secrets head-on. Only then can we rejoice and see the light within ourselves. Only then can it shine out onto the world.

HOW DO WE REALIZE OUR REWARDS?

The tragedies of life devour those who fall as their victims. The power to overcome hardships, death of loved ones, sickness, and the cruelties of the world lies deep within each of us. No human being lies separate from his own innateness to be master of his own affairs. The world is there to provide the fuel for each of us to burn away the parched crust of old ideas and pick up the sword of truth, to slay the dragons that lie at our doorstep. Be it said that each man, woman, and child must be the victor of their own life. Beware, for the obligatory help a loved one gives to another might be a hindrance to the salvation of both. True action comes from a true heart. A true heart comes from a search to find it. Purity can only be revealed if the din of the mind is quieted. Then life begins. We take heart; though the road is narrow and the rocks of life fall around us as we make our way to the mountaintop, our victory is assured. We are invincible. The road is long, but the reward is great.

HOW ARE PERCEPTIONS CHANGED?

Slowly, our journey proceeds down the path to the enlightenment of our mind and the realization of our soul. Sometimes, we rest along the way to regain our strength, to ready ourselves for what lies ahead of us. We listen to the same words from others, but now hear them differently. We see the same sights, but now notice more of their intricacies. We encounter the same situations, but now handle them with more calm and ease. Our intellect has sustained us, and we must honor it. Our mind tinkers with unruly thoughts, but now we forge a way to clear it of the needles that had continually pricked it and made it bleed with self-pity. Our world changes as our perceptions change. May we be thankful our road is hard; otherwise, we would have to be content to sit in comfortable ignorance. Now, we walk with our head higher and our inner voice whispering to us our true identity.

WHAT DOES THE CASTLE OF OUR HEART TELL US?

We build our castle in our heart. The mortar we use comes from the fears we have overcome. The flags that fly atop its mighty presence signify the freedom we have obtained. The path up to its entrance shows how we arrived to its mighty gate. We only let the drawbridge down for truthful thoughts and the sincerity of others. Surrounding our castle, the moat keeps the wiles of the world from intrusion. As our castle rests high on the side of a mountain, it grants us a vista of our own awareness. So we gather up our materials of stone and clay from the trials of our life. We lay them down on the firm foundation of faith. We endure the hardships and disappointments, as we build our castle brick by brick. Then, one day, we will turn around and see the castle of our heart.

WHERE IS OUR TRUE IDENTITY?

We let our spirit rise and express its true nature. Our body is truly a temple of holiness. As we clean our mind of negative thoughts, our essence manifests freely. Unencumbered, our life takes on a new meaning. We act naturally and without stress. We see the world with a bright clarity. Our judgment is sound, and our action is focused and powerful. This existence bears witness to an uncovering of the falseness that once surrounded us, like a cloud that gives way to the sun. Nothing has power over us unless we allow it. So we take our steps slowly, and are assured that when our journey completes, we stand firm in the realization of ourselves. We leave no stone unturned that needs to be released. We face all our fears, and life honors us; we are life, and life honors itself.

HOW DO WE MAKE FLOW IN LIFE'S CYCLE?

Into the depths of our soul, we reach for our true existence. Strain gives way to our heritage of freedom, and our days brighten with the hope of an even better tomorrow. The seasons fold into each other, and then come around to grace the earth once again. Each season displays its beauty, as do each day and each moment. By our own volition, we peel off the heaviness that weighs down our life and fall into the rhythm of life's natural beauty. Our season of despair fades and gives rise to a time of hope and promise. Our transition, which might seem slow, in reality falls into the natural order of who we are. We allow nature to have its way, and it bestows its lavish gifts upon us. As the winter snow melts and gives way to a flower's bud, so do we release ill will and unnecessary troubles for the promise of eternity in the moment. As the trees turn green and the flowers bloom, we realize the truth of ourselves and the vibrance of life. As the leaves color and fall to the ground, so must we be stricken bare and kneel to our Father. As the air becomes cold and the storms come, we hibernate within the essence of ourselves; from that strength, we weather any outcome. As the storms cease and the bees pollinate life, we once again grow more beautiful as we flow in life's cycle.

WHAT IS THE WAY TO STEP INTO LIFE?

We stop allowing the burdens of life to weigh down our hearts. We turn our mind to our freedom, and life's annoyances wither away. We find solace in our darkest hours, with the realization that life is just a passing moment, and we are eternal. As personalities attempt to grind us down, we give way to them and simply observe. In reality, they walk blindly and simply run into us. As we turn on the light of our mind and soul, we make our way around them. We let the moment sharpen our mind and enlighten us to the secrets of life. We walk with our head high and our step brisk with purpose. We know our way now. The path is clear. We set our mind with certainty of success and let our journey never end, but instead blossom with unending joy of the realization of ourselves.

HOW DO WE WITHSTAND THE EARTHQUAKES IN OUR LIFE?

The earthquakes keep coming, but we stand our ground. We feel the earth tremble, but we do not take flight. We stand and swerve with its movement. Rocks fall from the mountains above us, but we move to avoid their crush. Although somewhat bruised, we raise ourselves up and dust off the dirt from our clothes. Then we walk over to a pool of cool water and refresh ourselves. We can withstand the small shocks. We feel more strength and resilience than ever before. Gradually, we make our way up the mountain. We see the snowcapped summit awaiting us with its freshness and purity. Yes, we die to our old ways and uncover the new, as we walk proudly on our way.

WHAT DO WE NEED TO MASTER OUR MINDS?

Our capacity to achieve our goals depends on our willingness to expend the effort and the belief in ourselves that we can in fact accomplish them. The mind must be trained to obey our highest intentions. It waits on our bidding and unemotionally carries out our innermost desires. The truth of the matter lies in the fact that, in most cases, we pattern our mind to set ourselves up for failures and feelings of anxiety and want. However, life really *does* present us opportunities for freedom and abundant happiness. As we feed our mind visions of the accomplishments of our heart's true desires, it allows our world to change for the better. Gradually, through our own efforts, the physical realities manifest, fulfilling our desires. The only impediment to this process is our own belief that we cannot fulfill our own wishes. So, the task at hand is to reach into our heart for the true desire within us. We then bolster ourselves up with confidence, by encouraging and loving ourselves even at our weakest hour. We walk with the assurance that we have already achieved our goal. We stay focused and aware, so we can discern the best path. We are tenacious in our effort to release any negative thoughts and feelings based on outward appearances. Finally, we achieve a joy even kings and presidents will never know.

HOW IS OUR VICTORY ASSURED?

We are of good cheer, for the illumination of our mind sets the stage to our freedom. The mirage of deception is peeled back and displays the lies of the world with clarity. Our successes in this battle for our life have been great and admirable. They give us strength to forge ahead into the new arenas of engagement that await us. We set out in a full run, with all our strength, to conquer the fears that beleaguer our soul. We assure ourselves victory. We meet our darkest enemies head-on and defeat them. We stand tall in grace, and the dignity of our soul shines uninterrupted. We say: come, then, world. Show us your wares so we may vanquish them. We vow our determination will never die. We wrap ourselves in the faith of our achievements. Everlasting life is ours. Freedom beckons us with its sweet call. Peace fills us after each battle. Conflict dissipates with each new awareness. Subtly happiness fills us with an unending nourishment. We follow our path without deviation. We devote ourselves to our salvation. We stand, invincible to the trials of the world. We are steadfast. We are sure, and we are victorious. No one can take this from us. We vow our victory.

HOW DO WE LIVE LIFE FULLY?

These blessed moments nurse our soul, as calm and peace pour over us. The restlessness gives way to the power of assuredness of truth and the eternity of ourselves. We comfort ourselves with true expression and observe its beauty. By our own faith and courage, we walk proudly. As we earn our keep, our legs grow stronger and our stride becomes more natural. We do not strain, but instead observe the flow of life. The windows of our soul open to allow our light to stream forth. Our day becomes relaxed and effortless. We see our progress, and smile and acknowledge our rich heritage. So, patiently, we must wait for even greater rewards. We must become less demanding, more patient, and dive into the moment. Then, we won't miss anything. We will then have it all.

HOW DO WE PROGRESS INTO OUR NEW LIFE?

Glad tidings come our way. Our toil now sees its rewards, and our days ease, as we release our constant struggling. Enriched from our new experiences, we become emboldened. Our confidence builds. We encourage ourselves to take on our fears and conquer them. With our mighty sword of faith, we step forward into waters we once observed from the safety of the shoreline. Our mood gradually changes, as our awareness grows. Fear gives way to confidence. As we urge ourselves on, we set the stage for a new life, filled with the adventure of discovery instead of trepidation of the unknown. When the temptation of fears and anxieties arises, we tell ourselves of the joys of our new life. As time passes, we will no longer know the old ways. We stand in the moment, unattached, unafraid, and totally free. We sing like a bird, with great joy in our heart.

HOW ARE WE MEANT TO DISCOVER LIFE?

Our spirit rises, and hope in our heart sings with joy. With each passing moment, we feel our star shining with more brightness and clarity. The blessings we feel cannot be extinguished or dissipated. With awareness comes freedom. Emotional trappings fall off; they have nothing to hang on to. Life fills itself with the moment, and nothing else matters. Challenges still present themselves, but now a resolution is made more clear. With faith and confidence, fears wither away. They no longer intimidate and cause anxiety to rise and impede achievement. The brainwashing of our mind and its emotional crippling weaken. Now, we take over our life and steer its course. We walk with dignity and confidence. We take only what is ours and leave others what is rightfully theirs. Our Father's blessings *do* enrich us. We see them now. They uplift us and send us out to discover more and more of life.

WHY MUST WE TOIL SO?

The vast ocean of consciousness awaits being explored. It beckons us, like a soft breeze with the freshness of spring in the air. The delights of rewards lap upon the shores of our mind and touch our soul with a taste of heaven. Slowly, we awaken to the realities of life and watch ourselves in its play. Only through the toil laid upon our brow may we see the heaven that is ours. Even the thought of this gift humbles us. We bow our head to its mystery and mercy. As our ego's hold loosens, we grasp an awareness that shines so bright it lays out the once jumbled pieces of our life in order. So, let us toil and toil again. We want our freedom.

HOW DO WE ENTER INTO THE FLOW OF LIFE?

We smile, as the barriers of our life continue to decay, and we feel the strength of our own love begin to flow. Gradually, we step forward into our new life with confidence and vigor. Old trappings hold on, but their grip weakens; soon, their memory fades away. Our past experiences sometimes dance before our eyes and show us the formulation of the circumstances of our life. As we see them, we can understand ourselves without judgment. Our awareness grants us the vehicle to release the unwanted patterns of pain and anxiety, and also reveals the virtue we attained through our own efforts. As we step into ourselves, we express ourselves with more ease. Through our expression, we free ourselves. Our creativity flows, and therefore our confidence rises. We engage a new cycle in our life. It opens to a natural rhythm, and we are in tune with the universal forces.

HOW ARE REWARDS GAINED?

The mystery of life displays itself and opens its doors to us. With simplicity, we step forward and enjoy its fruits. Its pastures are greener, and its skies are graced with a blue color that takes our breath away. As our fear dissipates, our life takes on new meaning. The playing field levels, and our walk strengthens. Gradual awareness is the key, and determination assures our success. As the cloak of darkness falls from around us, the heaviness that weighs upon us lifts. Freedom sings in our heart. Answers come, and life tickles our nose with its sweetness. We journey on unhampered. We express our wants and fulfill our needs. We see with clarity the good and bad in others. Life comes to us, and our struggle becomes less. So, we continue to unlearn to see. We continue to face fears and be free. We know if we never give up, life will reward us beyond our wildest dreams.

WHAT IS TRUE STRENGTH?

Our spirit rings with a newfound freedom, and we continue on our way. The cloak of ignorance and fear persistently veils our sight, although its weight has lightened. We throw it back, and yet we remain entangled. Finally, we pull it off from our head, and it falls lifelessly to the ground. Our Father's strength has brought us to this point, and our Father's strength will bring us home. We walk the long road to our freedom, and it cannot be any other way. Where once we despaired, we now have hope. We move from doubt and confusion to confidence and clarity. Patiently and with absolute resolve, we assure ourselves of success. There is no arrival; that would be limiting. There is only more and more happiness. So we proceed, step by step, to earn our rewards. We walk in humility, yet hold our head high. Glory to our Father; He is our strength and our love.

FOR WHAT, THEN, MUST WE BE GRATEFUL?

Gratefully, we step forward into our new life and reap our rewards. Heaven has waited patiently for us, and now we come to meet it. Gradually, ever so gradually, we pull off the veil of deceptions and falsehoods that have ensnared our mind. As we grow in the awareness of ourselves, we see with ever more clarity the world in which we live. The truth surely *does* set us free. As the same situations arise, we address them with more and more confidence. We see our way through or around the obstacles in our life. We grow stronger every day, and learn how to love ourselves with no conditions. Only we can walk this path; it is ours alone. We give thanks for our friends who guide us along the way, however, the steps are ours to take. As we walk along on our journey, we feel the joy of life, for life surely is a gift. We are very grateful for the opportunity to be alive.

WHAT DOES CLARITY REVEAL TO US?

Rich blessings pour forth and bring sparkle to our life. New clarity brings us peace. As we see with less burdened eyes, our life takes on new meaning. We walk with a lighter step and a surer stride. Anger falls off, as our view of life becomes more clear. The evils of the world craft themselves in many forms. It is only through self-realization that we can see their masquerade and then discard them. They no longer pose a threat. Through our own perceptions, we set the course of our life. Nothing can stop us but ourselves. Faith instills us with the strength to carry on. It is truly blasphemy, not to believe in our Holy Father. He is our Light. He is our love. He is us, and we are Him. He is eternal, and in this realization, the truth rings loud. Humbly, we bow our head and give thanks. Without Him, we can do nothing. With Him, we walk in joy and peace.

HOW DO REALIZATIONS BRING FREEDOM?

Freedom rings out as it reverberates from our soul. We awaken to our new life and give thanks in this moment. We steer our course down the road of our destined journey. The tears of weeping turn into tears of joy. Step by step, we climb to the mountaintop of love, which is us. Our heart warms and then expands, as we nurture ourselves. We can be of no value, unless we love ourselves. We can have no happiness, unless we listen to the soft whisper that comes from within ourselves. We have looked at life through a dirty window. We scrub as we must, the film that clouded our life, and it gradually dissipates. If we hurry, we keep smearing it around. If we are patient, we clean it away, and it never returns. We are so blessed to have come so far, but journey on we must. That is what we need to do to set our soul completely free. We are eternal and unlimited. We want to realize, to realize.

IN WHAT WAY CAN WE CONQUER THE DRAGON OF UNRULY THOUGHTS?

The tedium of our busy mind wears us down and takes our much-needed energy. We allow realizations to come, but they no longer need to be accompanied by recycling the same thoughts. What is done is done, and what will be will be. Our task is to ride the wave of the moment, and not to falter in this endeavor. We forgive ourselves now for our past transgressions of feelings of ineptitude and lack of self-confidence. We free ourselves from the burdens of our mind, running events that never happened or never will happen. Our life beckons us, right here and right now, to feel it, touch it, and embrace it. The thief of distracting thoughts robs us of living a full and rich life. Our time has come; by conquering the unruly habit of runaway thoughts, we can step further into ourselves and a life of creativity, wonder, and joy. Life is for those who truly, truly love themselves. If we truly love ourselves, we no longer need to cause ourselves pain.

Mental pain deteriorates the body, which needs to operate with vigor and health in this physical world. O' Father, give us the fortitude to slay this dragon in our mind. Let us see Your light, and let it wash the recurring nonsense from our mind. Let us stand up to our fears and walk courageously through our life, unhampered by extraneous and lingering thoughts.

WHAT IS THE WAY TO RELEASING UNWANTED THOUGHTS?

Graciously, we accept our newfound freedom. Our life levels out, and we walk an easier path. Our rewards sprout up, like beautiful flowers strewn across an open field. The light of the sun shines on us, and we feel invigorated from its glow. The softness of the earth comforts our step, and we feel in tune to nature's bounty. We do the same things, but now feel a sense of promise. As life becomes more clear, we feel a sense of confidence and calm. As harshness rises up and confronts us, we see it more for its true representation. As we grow stronger, it falters. It never had power. It is we that gave it power. The fight is not over, but in fact, there is no fight. Instead, we continue to drop the years of bad habits that haunted our existence and kept us hostage in our own mind. To break the remaining bad habits of our negative and reoccurring thoughts, we pray. We bolster our confidence and rest in the assurance of our success. Step by step, we walked this far, and, step by step, we discard the nonsense that no longer needs a place in our mind.

WHAT IS THE WAY TO SELF-REALIZATION?

Thy grace o' Father fills us and spills out into our life. The promises You made are eternally kept. You point the way through the darkness to those that open their eyes and look. Blindness is not physical, but instead comes from our own minds. Through our intuition, we realize; through our minds, we discern our thoughts and act upon them.

So suffice it to say, to live a life of wonder and joy, we must tame our mind and use it for the tool it is meant to be. We can reason with it. We can decipher problems with it. We can create with it. The goal here is to first quiet the mind, and then direct it for Your purpose. The intuition sparks the thought in the mind. The mind must understand its meaning. The will must decide what to do with the thought. Determination and perseverance will bring the thought into action and then into fruition. Then, and only then, can we feel alive and fulfilled. By trusting and loving ourselves, we charge our life with so much energy, the only outcome must be success. Dignity comes from this path, and that is the result of self-realization. No other way exists.

HOW DO WE REALIZE OUR ONENESS WITH OUR FATHER?

No guarantees exist along the road to freedom. No hand lifts us up when we have fallen down. No progress comes, unless we alone want to succeed. True friends stand, ready to point the way. A loving spouse comforts us. However, our journey stands before us and beckons us. Our heart guides us on which way to turn. Our strength grows with each step we take. Let us hear. Let us see. Let us touch the essence of life. As we discipline our mind, we become more masterful in our ways. We can see the manifestation of more and more true action. As we reach more deeply into our soul, we find the riches we have been looking for. Our rewards come, but they are known only to us. They soothe our soul and give us peace as we move through each moment. We must settle our mind and let it rest. We must trust ourselves enough to take each moment as it comes. We must attend to our well-being as we allow ourselves the happiness that we are. Our True Self waits to be uncovered and released. Let us make peace with and love ourselves with the essence of who we really are. Our spirit is eternal. Its life is manifested in this body to learn the lessons that will make us grow and realize ourselves. O' dear Father, let us unfold the real us and sit at Your side in the garden of happiness and love. Let us hear Your soft whisper and feel Your caress. Let us know the oneness of being You.

WHAT MUST WE DO TO BE AT PEACE?

Happily, we move on with our life. As we take on a truer course, we feel an easiness and calm. We commit to a restful mind. We turn ourselves over to our new life. We no longer need to pretend what might happen or what should have happened. Just as we choose to crawl out of a hole of vast darkness, we now choose to release our mind of its extraneous running, which bears no meaning and no value. These trappings of our mind weigh on our body and cause it a tenseness that leaves it weary. Our true test is to control our thoughts and direct them toward right action. The ego runs our mind with old feelings of our childhood's inadequacies. We now release our past and walk courageously into our future. We rise to each moment and embrace it with our whole heart. No longer must we be a slave to a wandering mind that serves up fantasies. O' Father, may we master our thoughts and see You more clearly. May we be at peace and lay in the comfort of Your arms.

HOW DO WE FREE OURSELVES AND OTHERS?

The stark realities of life reveal themselves to us and teach us what we need to know about ourselves. Pure innocence can survive in this world, but it must be totally aware of itself. Naivety falters; it cannot withstand or bend to the travesties of life. Ignorance continually displays its ugly head to cast doubt and confusion. This is all it can do; that is its essence. We stand stronger today than we did yesterday, and we give thanks for our growing awareness every day. As we see more of truth, it naturally sets us free to a higher, more abundant life. We no longer need to carry the load of the slovenly and lazy. With our new sight, we determine an altruistic method to carry out our deeds. Each of us must accept their responsibility and put forth the effort to accomplish their goals. If this does not happen, discord occurs. So, through our newfound freedom and insight, we deem a proper action to carry ourselves proudly in the essence of who we really are. May we reflect ourselves with such dignity that the world will no longer lean on us, but instead see the light within itself or choose to walk back into its own darkness. Life is for living, not wallowing in the fear of retribution or the prideful sin of never allowing others to find their own way.

HOW DO WE COMMIT TO HAPPINESS?

Very deep within us lies the answer to our life. We must trust in our own urgings and follow their strong yet subtle prompts. No matter what the present conditions appear to be, the reality of who we are and what we commit ourselves to accomplish are all that matters. We must believe, truly believe with all our heart, the promptings of our soul. We must commit without waiver to what our heart lovingly tells us. We must believe with our whole being and resolve with all our strength to experience our journey with abounding happiness and a joy that can never be extinguished. Every negative thought we put down and disturbing emotion we release brings us closer to home. We then see ourselves and gaze upon the open door to our Father, who lives inside us. We must rest our mind for true sight to come. We must calm the storms of our emotions before we can lay down in the restful bliss our soul yearns for.

HOW IS OUR SOUL FREED?

Life's journey calls us, and with its beckoning, we pick up our cross and carry it to our everlasting freedom. It is only by bearing the burdens of life and then discarding them that we can finally lift up our head and realize who we are. As we unlearn the ingrained habits and patterns we have accumulated throughout our life, we step out of the gates of hell. We become more aware of our surroundings and our own being. We become more immersed in life, real life. No lies exist in our True Self. Only truth reigns; illusions do not exist. We must command our own course and steer ourselves through the troubled waters of life. Avoidance is not the answer.

We must face the blemishes of our life with courage and compassion for ourselves. Our mind is the vehicle to our freedom. We must control it and discard all the gnawing thoughts that continually linger on. No value comes from perpetually running thoughts. Peace only comes from the stillness that rests in the mind. Discipline is the tool to control our thoughts, and this releases us from the weight of worry and any doubts that may attempt to lie down in a cozy corner of our mind. We gain energy from our past victories, and now see ourselves as we set out on this newest task. To reveal our soul, we must lighten our mind. As we lighten our mind, the negative emotions we harbor will have nothing to hang onto, so they will dissipate. The positive energy of who we are will be left to manifest itself in creative ways, unhampered by any inhibitions or fears. Our life then must be clear, pure, and whole. So we make our choice to free our mind, and in doing so, we free our soul.

HOW IS OUR MIND TRANSFORMED?

The goodness we possess does not waiver in and out in a fleeting moment. Instead, it sits, steadfast and absolute. It is our perceptions that are colored by our thoughts and emotions, which promote the illusion of an unstable existence. The mind is a powerful tool, yet it is *just* a tool. Free will is the essence of who we are, and the mind takes its orders by decisions we make. Thought patterns become entrenched from our life's experiences, as well as from our past lives. They form a picture of our current events and what we think life will look like in the future. Our free will, coupled with the determination to drop old, useless thought patterns, opens our life to abundant blessings beyond our wildest dreams. As we rest quietly and hear our inner voice whisper its secrets to us, we begin to understand more of the mysteries of life. They lie beyond a soft veil that covers them from our sight. They wait there as they always have, resting in eternity. Life beckons us to live it, and live it we must. Step by step and thought by thought, we transform our mind and change our life to manifest our good.

WHAT IS LIFE'S TEST?

The test of everyday living reflects back to us who we really are. It provides us a true reflection of our progress in an exacting measure of what we need to work on and overcome. With ever more clarity, we see the world for what it is, and it provides us the freedom we knew was ours, but did not know how to obtain. The mind is an incredible instrument of intelligence and power. One person's thoughts can sway world events for many centuries. As we train our mind to dissolve its old, useless patterns, we then can change our life for years to come. We can be stuck in darkness for a lifetime, or we can drop our ignorance and walk on this earth with the dignity of a free human being. The choice rests with ourselves. The more we wipe away, the more we see of our soul. This encourages us and sends us down our path to an enlightened life. Our road is our own, and that is the most difficult path we can take. It is also the most rewarding. It provides us the gems of self-confidence, strength, and the love of ourselves. It reveals our very soul to us.

WHAT IS TRUE CONFIDENCE?

Confidence is the key to our peace of mind. Confidence comes from us facing our fears and exposing their nothingness. Our ego spins scenarios in our mind of events that might happen or events where we think we should have spoken or acted differently. This thinking reflects a lack of self-confidence. It echoes doubt and leaves the present moment without life. Reality rests in the now;

by our embracing the present, we can really see ourselves. No time exists in the present, for eternity lives there. For us to live in eternity, we must drop our fears and walk courageously with who we are right now. Step by step, we must embrace and love ourselves, no matter our circumstances. We see ourselves changing from a frightened child to a compassionate, loving adult, who continually grows with new awareness. The sinking feeling that used to accompany our life has weakened and continues to dissipate. Confidence means being true to ourselves and allowing ourselves the right to be strong, vibrant, and in charge of our life. We now let the thoughts go that drain our energy, and instead embrace our life right now.

HOW DO WE EXPERIENCE A TASTE OF HEAVEN?

Our heart calms, and we breathe more easily. We taste a drop of heaven, and we want to dip our cup in its cool water and fill ourselves up. We see the changes in our life, as it runs more smoothly and with less struggle. Only through our own volition do we continue to release ourselves from the debilitating thoughts that cripple our mind and leave us weak and ineffective.

Our thoughts and their patterns were sewn in our mind in our early childhood. They seek to hang on and hamper us from the joys and fulfillment of life. Our steps on this journey have been many, and the road now widens and levels out to meet us. We see the reflection of ourselves in our circumstances and watch ourselves hang onto old ways, as we move forward to the new beginnings of our life. Therefore, this is the time when we must be most tender with ourselves, more tender than a mother with her newborn child. Through this love, we can reach into the eternity of ourselves and rest in our own being, knowing who we truly are. With this knowledge, we can trust ourselves implicitly and walk in the Garden of Eden, never to be thrown out. Our awareness will guide us, and our attention and devotion to our Father will grant us the grace and strength to dive deeper into our soul and wash ourselves in the coolness of heaven's waters.

HOW IS HEAVEN EARNED?

Confrontation shakes us, and, in its wake, leaves us with feelings that are disruptive and upsetting. We admit the picture of the world we see is not clear, although we have rubbed much dirt from the window of our perception. Our frustration also rises when other peoples' blindness dictates their thoughts and actions, either through their own ignorance or through calculated, deceptive ways. Even the small drops of peoples' discord affect us like tiny pebbles that land in a pond and create circles from their impact. We feel a great sense of achievement for our life's journey, and we proclaim our good. Through our own efforts, we walk more proudly and with more confidence than we have ever done before. We see the task at hand as our major challenge. We have cleared the mental garbage from our mind, so now our greatest demon looms in front of us and sneers at us with contempt. We have crawled from the depths of the hell in our mind to reach a point where the light of dawn reaches out to show us the battlefield before us. To root out our fears, once and for all, we must admit they lie within us and face them with resolve. Our thoughts of low self-confidence, coupled with an ignorance of the world and its deceptive ways, leave us trapped in fearful anxiety. But now, as we are loosening the burdens of our soul, our true strength rises up. Although we do not yet realize our true, infinite strength, we do see the changes in our life that we brought about by our own merit to *empower* ourselves and take control of our life. So our only choice is to engage ourselves in battle against the devils that choose to keep us trapped in frustration and despair. Freedom still stands as our goal; we cannot waiver. Heaven must be earned.

WHO IS THE PRODIGAL SON?

The ego hangs on with the tenacity of a frightened young child. It is spoiled in its ways and seeks the comfort of familiarity. It gets violently upset when it is not in control, and it works its devious methods to always have its own way. Therefore, growth shakes it to its foundation, and it digs in and hangs on with everything in its power. It hides in the darkness of itself; it feels safe there. It causes us pain and grief to keep us trapped in our wounds and self-pity. It causes us confusion, so we will not take corrective action. It boasts us up, only to let us down on its roller coaster of emotions. It ruled our life, and now, we say no more. We vow to relieve ourselves of its ills. We vow to cast off its cloak of deception. We vow to drop the weight of its stones. We vow to face it head-on and tell it goodbye. We now take charge. We make our own decisions. We rule our life. We set our course. We enjoy our fruits. We love and honor ourselves. We walk through the gates of heaven, and our Father is there to greet us. We are the prodigal son who has come home. We rejoice!

WHAT IS THE RHYTHM OF LIFE?

In the ebb and tide, we flow. After the violent emotional storms, the strong winds in our mind blow. Next, a soft breeze flows over us, and we rest in a peaceful state. As we delve even deeper into our past, the cycle starts once again. From the very beginning, we are. Our spiritual path in this life was designed to give us long-sought answers. As we turn over each rock on the path of our life, it reveals to us what we need to know. No rock must remain unturned; the alternative is to continue to carry them. As we drop the weight from our heart and our mind, we move through the ebb and flow. Life truly does reflect back to us what is inside us. It does not lie, but instead provides lesson after lesson to free us from self-imposed hurt and the deception of unworthiness. Miracles occur every day, and they are a reflection of ourselves. They twinkle like stars across the sky and light up our life, one by one. Arrows of ignorance, deception, and laziness that bear down on us help us to put on our armor of truth, courage, and steadfastness as we proceed to our goal of freedom. After every storm, there is a calm, and after every calm, there is a storm. This is the rhythm of life: ebb and flow, ebb and flow.

WHAT TAKES US DOWN THE PATH TO PEACE?

After each victory comes a sense of self-confidence. Then, once again, some small matter runs through our mind and magnifies itself to an immense proportion. This is a lifetime habit. It comes from circumstances, family, and emotional upsets in our early childhood. These self-made emotional overloads send us into a cycle of an over-active mind, emotional upheaval, and physical reaction of nervousness and weakness in our body. Now, as we continue to pull the veil from around our head that cloaks our vision, we can see the cause and effect of our life. Through our awareness, we set ourselves free from the daunting cycle that keeps putting us back to a place of low self-esteem and low self-confidence. It is in our power to break the cycle that artificially impedes our full potential. We invite the guests of courage, determination, self-confidence, and poise to rest in our mind. This leaves no room for weakness, self-doubt, and self-pity to remain. Our task relies on our free will and the determination we muster to drop the tenacious habits of our childhood and instead walk forward as the intelligent, talented, and dignified individuals we are. The good grace of our Father fills us. Our attention turns from self-pity to success in our life. Our journey has been long, but our fortitude and determination have taken us far down our path to self-realization and freedom. The devil tempts us with distractions and feelings of self-doubt, as we step forward into the uncharted waters of our life. We now stand, ready and firm. Our victories are assured, and the peace and harmony that have made their way into our life provide us the faith to step forward. Faith in ourselves, faith in our Father, faith in our Benefactor's guidance whisk away the cloudy, murky sights we see before us. We must step through the deceptions of our life and reveal them for what they are. This is the only way. We raise our head high, step forward, and claim our victory of the realization of our eternal and True Self.

HOW DO WE PLAY ON THE FIELD OF LIFE?

Our treasures stand before us, and all we need to do is pick them up and drop them in our pocket. We stand at the threshold of our life with a clean uniform and a destiny we know not yet. Our heart assures us success, and our mind wants to look back, but we now look forward with confidence and assurance. Our weight is lighter, and our actions more sure. We have walked through the tunnels of the caves of our mind into the light of day. We see the green grass of the fields before us, and feel the radiance of the sun as a cloud gives way. The playing field has become more even, and we come with our bat in hand and a new glove that is eager to try its turn. As we step out to the plate, we feel the nervousness in our stomach and sweat on our brow. We stand ready, with our feet planted firm as we focus in the moment at hand. This relaxes us and we settle into our stance. As the pitch comes toward us, we move forward with our swing, and with this action, we are in the game.

WHAT ARE LIFE'S BLESSINGS?

Life's purpose is to grow. Creation is the essence of life. Nature's cycle begins with the manifestation of birth, then a maturation occurs, and finally death ends the cycle. A natural progression exists for all nature. It is only the human that fights this process. However, struggling against nature and life itself is a futile endeavor. No other true way presents itself but to learn and grow from life's experiences. So, from a true perspective, life is grand; to experience it fully provides blessings of untold happiness. A fearful outlook generates self-pity. A courageous view of life grants an ever-expanding awareness of oneself and uncovers a world full of wonder. We realize now that we cannot tread lightly; that offers no rewards. We cannot move forward with recklessness and haste; that ensnares us and pulls us down. However, when we relax and listen, we can hear the truth within our heart. When we follow its whisper, we flow down the river of life to our freedom. When we stumble and fall, we nurture ourselves. We encourage ourselves to carry on and never give up on our quest of life itself. By accepting who we really are and overcoming life's obstacles, we walk into a glory that outshines our wildest dreams. Our blessings are great. We are comforted and at peace.

WHAT IS A GENTLE WARRIOR?

Tension rises up from within us for no good reason. It is from a persistent habit that causes no value, but, instead, unnecessary heartache and deterioration of our body. We play victim in our mind and then defend ourselves. We take what people say to our heart, and then allow ourselves to blow it up to monumental proportions. We see ignorance, nonsense, and downright cruelties and manipulation and then take them on as an affront to ourselves. We say to ourselves, "How can they be that way?" Well, they just are; it must be of no concern to us.

Now, as we train ourselves to let these feelings go, we regain ourselves. We feel our energy rising and our strength growing. This victory tells us in truth of the great accomplishments we have achieved on our journey. We waver less and move more freely. Therefore, we can say without a doubt that the hesitancy has started its dissent and confidence rises swiftly to take its place. Oh! This is a beautiful realization; it brings us a peace we cannot describe with words. We see the task before us to curb this devil of worry that causes us turmoil, discord, and physical harm. However, our awareness reveals the truth of self-inflicted weaknesses. From this awareness, we forge ahead to eradicate them from our mind. Father, where have we been? Truly, this prodigal son wants to come home. So we must conquer the obstacles that lay before us; in this way, we clean our mind and soul from the rubbish that besets it. Freedom comes from faith, and the strength and determination to achieve it. Oh! What a mighty warrior rests inside our soul. From this peace, the Gentle Warrior reveals itself to us.

HOW DO WE HONOR OUR FATHER?

We let our Father's gracious Spirit fill us up and wash our mind of any of its trumped-up troubles. We must not give these demons strength or encourage their continuation. As we relax and concentrate on ourselves and the essence of our holiness, all else falls off. We feel pure, content, and unhampered in creativity. We just are, and we just do. So the truth of who we are tells us we are our Father's instrument. We are His manifestation, and we carry His life. Our talents are God-given; they evoke a goodness that enriches us and wakes us up to who we are.

As we follow our destiny, we settle into a peacefulness. Our awareness builds upon itself and provides us the stepping stones to ever more happiness. If we are in a hurry, we cannot realize the fact that we are eternal. In eternity, there is no rushing. There is nowhere to rush to and nothing to achieve. The trials of the world will always exist, as long as the world exists. These challenges of life, if used wisely, open doors to the pearls of wisdom, peace, and everlasting happiness that live inside our soul.

Heaven is in our midst. It resides there, waiting for us to show up and lie down at its feet. It urges us to free our mind and calm our emotions. It tells us to accept our uniqueness and honor the holiness we really are. We need to make a choice. Do we grovel on the earth in misery and self-inflicted pain, or do we accept our fate to stand up to the devils in our mind and banish them forever? This is our choice. Yes, only fear and love exist. We pray, and the courage comes; its wings carry us through the clouds and darkness to the land of triumph and joy. We must resurrect ourselves and stand firm and vigilant in freedom. Dear Father, take us in Your arms. Let us see Your light, and provide us the strength and courage to walk into the "Land of Milk and Honey" You so graciously offer us. We are Your children. We see Your smiling face, and we thank You for the blessing of being alive.

HOW IS THE TRUTH MANIFESTED IN US?

Inscribed in our mind lies a vision of who we really are. A notion in our heart urges us, with firmness and softness, to set out from our shell of comfort into a world of challenges designed to give us our freedom. Our body feels lighter, although our mind is still flooded with thoughts. Our spiritual pace displays to us a rise in our energy, as we move more naturally. A harness still lies on our back, but no longer chokes our spirit. Our only way is through the difficulties of life that we created or were given to us by circumstances.

We hear our voice, and although it sounds weak, it says the words we always wanted to say. Truth cannot be covered or denied. It must be spoken and acted upon. The consequences of not honoring the truth spell disaster. The words "True to ourselves" then take on a special meaning. They provide the key to unexplored lands of our life. They allow us to walk free and love ourselves, with no conditions attached. Truth is absolute. Faith allows us the sight to know it's there. Our will gives us the opportunity to choose it. Our determination takes us to it. Then the truth washes over us and in us and is us. We must be true to ourselves.

HOW DO WE SING OUR OWN SONG?

Our spirit is filled today with righteousness and joy. We see our path before us, and it holds blessings so rich our mind cannot comprehend their magnitude. We see our way made clear, so we can now begin our ascent. Our legs are strong enough for the climb, and our hearts point us up toward the steep precipice. Our feet are steady, and somehow we feel an old comfort and familiarity as we embark. Our training prepared us for the events that lie before us. Our soft realizations of ourselves provide us a serenity accompanied by an assured confidence. We rest where are, see the beauty there, and accept it. Whatever we have is good, and we honor ourselves by accepting our gifts bestowed on us from life itself. This is our place—in this moment, as we glance up at the sky. We hear a bird sing in the distance, and then again notice the silence as it rests. Now, we sing our song, and when we are done, we rest.

HOW DO WE TRAVERSE THE SEASONS OF OUR LIFE?

Our spirit awakens to a new life that is different from our past, and the landscape we once knew takes on a different season. The mountains, although they still call us, are not as looming and steep. Subtleties that once escaped our glance now show themselves to us with their fine beauty. Our life paints itself before our eyes and gives us pause. All the people we once thought we knew now seem so different. Their faults and imperfections did always exist, which stretched our tolerance into frustration and eventually anger. Instead of seeing with our eyes, we now see with our heart. Our gradual acceptance of life opens our heart to reconciliation with ourselves and all those we deal with, whether at work or with our family. We truly feel a change in the seasons of our mind and heart.

From the deadness in our soul, which was barren from a long dark winter, we watched the roots take hold and get nurtured from the heavy rains of our tears. As we are able to raise our head and straighten our body, we relieve ourselves of the burdens of our many years. We watch the small buds of happiness push through the ground into the light of our Father's sun, which tenderly nourishes these delicate flowers that begin to fill themselves with life. The long winter has given way to the roots that, in the spring, grow the beginnings of the manifestation of our new life, serving us well as we build our strength and take on our duties, making us even stronger, bending, and molding us into the beauty of who we really are.

HOW DO WE PRAY TO YOU, FATHER?

Heaven has laid its arms around us and gently soothes our soul with its grace. Strength can only come from holiness, and holiness can only come from the bounty of our Father's grace. We do nothing on our own, because we need our Father's gifts in all we do. With His blessings, He has given us power over all our destiny and allows us the freedom to explore Him. So thank You, dear Father, for Your righteousness, kindness, and love. Only through Your grace can we bestow it to others and enrich Your abundance. O' heavenly Father, may the angels sing Your praise. Let us all kneel down before You and worship who You really are, knowing that we share in Your bounty of goodness, strength, and everlasting love.

O' heavenly Father, fill us with Your abundant love. Guide us down the path to peace and abundant prosperity. Nurture us with Your soft voice of truth, and provide us the faith to conquer our fears and overcome our adversities. Let Your light illuminate our mind with only positive, constructive thoughts. Fill our activity with Your presence, and watch over us when we sleep at night. Let us sing Your praise with enthusiasm and feel Your pure love emanated from our soul. O' dearest Father and Almighty ruler, we bow down before You and await Your message and Your call. Holy, holy, holy is Your name.

HOW DO WE ENJOY LIFE?

From the depths of our soul, we feel the need to allow life to open up to us its hidden mysteries. Through our own faith, the road to peace widens and shows a clear way to the righteousness that was once hidden inside our heart. Our life takes on a new direction, as we allow ourselves the passage to express our true feelings and desires. It is true, life cannot be denied to those who really want to display their God-given talents. Happiness can only come from that expression.

Submerged within the deep recesses of our souls lies our True Self. It is only from our own free will that we allow ourselves to emerge and thereby join ourselves with life and an awareness of the Father Himself. The mysteries of life surround us; to uncover their secrets evokes a happiness that transcends words and enriches our soul with the ever-increasing knowledge of itself. The sacred teachings passed on from generation to generation have no meaning unless they are realized by ourselves. Words fall flat, in an attempt to instruct us in the true meaning of life. Only through self-realization can life be opened up and experienced. The road is solitary, and sometimes dark and ominous, but through faith and determination, the light of day does dawn. The fears that once seemed so dreadful and immense give way to happiness and peace. The formula is the same. We must listen to our heart and start on our way. Although we stumble and fall again and again, we must rise up and continue with pure determination. Only then does the birds' song sound sweeter, the blue sky with its clouds become more beautiful, and life itself holds out its hand to us as we walk easily on our way.

HOW IS HAPPINESS REALIZED?

Forever do we see our fate—to grow, to love, and to be at ease with all there is. The earthly life teaches hard lessons so we can truly understand. It turns its ignorance up to a high volume with a voracious intensity, in the name of power. Our heart needs to settle down; all is truly right with us. We have stepped from the shadows into the light and find true happiness that was long hidden deep within us. It lay dormant, waiting for us to claim its preciousness. Life is truly too short to dither it away on self-doubt and fear. They have had their way to rob us blind from the blessing of confidence and the achievements that it make possible. Now that we have embarked on a new life, our lack of patience still haunts us. We must then tame this devil and let it loose, so we can enjoy the fruits we have so dutifully earned.

The rich life unfolds to us, step by step. It is not in a magic instant that the world is now all right and bends to our will. Instead, moment by moment, as our awareness reveals to us the simple truths of life, we feel the weight recede from our shoulders and experience happiness that builds on itself with unending expansion. Our time has come to shed our shell and reveal ourselves to the world. This can only come by loving ourselves and being true to our own heart. Even those we love and those that love us must know the truth. We cannot please their every whim and give in to even the small things if it compromises us from being true to ourselves. Our happiness comes to us now. It cannot be denied. We deserve it. We want it and pay the price to realize its beauty as it lights up our life with the Father Himself.

MAY WE PRAY TO YOU, OUR HEAVENLY FATHER?

Our Father has reached down and touched our brow with such tenderness and love, our heart shudders at just the thought of it. The devils we fear the most roar and taunt us, but our Father stands with us with calm strength, as our sight becomes more clear with His vision. The reality that lies before our eyes sets us free; the reflection of our True Self shines out to light our way. Our Father sends His angels to guide us along our path to greater awareness, so we do not stray or become distracted with earthly desires. Each step is our own, but each breath we take comes from Him. He surrounds us with our friends on this earth plane and also with those in spirit who are there to help us. We are sustained with the support of all those around us. They nurture us with their love and comfort us when we falter.

O' heavenly Father, let us hear Your voice with more clarity. Let us do Your work with more cheerfulness. Let us kneel down before Your Almighty presence. Father, Your beauty is beyond words, beyond thought, beyond reason. The heaven You provide us humbles us. The joy you give so freely brings us happiness that transcends all emotion. Our place is with You, O' Holy Father. We beseech You to give us the strength to do Your will.

HOW DO WE HEAL OUR RELATIONSHIPS?

We need to stop demanding people need to change to suit our whims. Happiness is not dependent upon the whole world being aright for it to descend upon us and bless our life. Acceptance is the key to fullness. We have no right to expect anyone to change their ways to suit us. We must instead accept ourselves with all our faults, and honor ourselves with all of our imperfections. By doing so, we honor the other person. We see them for who they really are. We must walk hand-in-hand with our neighbors with the same respect we have for ourselves. The insecurities each of us hangs onto causes the strife and disharmony in any relationship. So, as we look inside, we must express our true feelings, not only to ourselves, but to those around us. Then, and only then, will harmony come. The slate must be swept clean of words that have never been said and feelings that have never been expressed.

So how do we change a behavior between two people that has been locked into a pattern for so long? The answer, we already know. Step by step, the knots must be untied, with patience. Those silent thoughts must be spoken out loud, and those feelings long suppressed must be brought into the light. Heaven can only come when all is forgiven. Only then will calmness take the place of strain and release us from the bondage that does not let us fully realize ourselves.

WHAT STEPS DO WE TAKE TO FREE OURSELVES?

Just to let life simply come at times seem so insurmountable. Yet, just the glimmer of our Father's hand makes us feel it is so achievable.

Our past successes light the way for our future ones. There is no other world but our own, which encompasses our thoughts and feelings. An enlightened soul leads an enlightened life. The steps to a flowing life seem at times cumbersome, strenuous, and downright grueling. But the only way to our rewards is by facing any obstacle or fear keeping us from what we so want from the depths of our soul. Our Father shows the way for all of us to pull ourselves from the depths of the burning fires of hell into the cool calm of who we really are.

Our life has carried with it a suppression and dominance that have caused an anxiety to ripple our body with stress, leaving us forlorn in a world we wander, aimlessly and lost. It is only through our own will and determination that our Father so graciously and lovingly provides us the courage and guidance to walk out of the hell that cages us and burns us into a passive submission. One step at a time, we make our journey to where we exist not only today but in this very moment. Now, only through our own volition and determination, do we proceed to continue to face our life with all it offers.

O' Holy Father, guide us along our destined path. Keep us safe. Fill our soul with Your abundant love and strength, and provide us the wisdom to navigate our way through the trials that lie before us. May we forgive all past transgressions and walk proudly into our future to feel the calmness and peace You so graciously provide us; it is our heritage.

WHAT DOES IT MEAN TO STEP FORWARD IN OUR RELATIONSHIPS?

The grace of our Father lightens our heart and takes our breath away. The magnitude of His love is beyond the comprehension of our mind. The small steps we take toward freedom bring us jubilation and unending encouragement. The journey that once seemed so dark and unsurmountable has given way to an easiness in living, with a guarantee of better and better days as we eventually step into eternity. With union in our Father, our confidence builds. The foundation of who we are resounds with more strength and vibrance as our awareness brings it into existence. The trials of our loved ones are just that. They toil in the thorns of their own minds as we do in ours, but through our own strength, growth, and determination, we can provide them real comfort.

It is not through worry that we comfort or nurture. It is not from placating and being amiable that we find the trappings of a relationship. Instead, we must profess with honesty what's in our heart and be willing to take the consequences and ultimately the risk of losing those we hold close to us. But what do we have, if we must tiptoe around to keep peace so empty conversations might occur and real feelings are not addressed? Our life and all lives must absolutely be lived in truth, honesty, and conviction to realize our true nature. No way exists to become aware of the gift of our Father, unless we are willing to sacrifice all for our Father's love. Then, and only then, will He fully reveal Himself to us.

WHAT IS STRENGTH?

We must stand up, be strong, and weather the tests that lie in front of us. These trials beat down the doors that lock our mind and let us walk merrily out into the world, armed with new awareness. Our courage conquers any lies or masquerades that veil themselves in order to control our soul. Our Father's strength lies within all of us. Our solemn covenant with our Father assures confidence that our will to realize our goodness and love is met with our Father's gracious and loving heart, which binds us forever to Him. Let it be said, we all take up our cross and carry it to the doors of eternity. As we accept our True Self in totality, the need to carry burdens simply fades away into the nothingness from which it came. May our Father's glory shine on all of us, and may we all realize the true nature of who we really are.

HOW IS OUR IGNORANCE RELEASED?

Our soul longs for the passage of time to cease and eternity to spread its glorious arms around us. The vastness inside us lies dormant, in anticipation of being released. The transformation of our mind sets us free to explore even deeper the mysteries of the world, as we unravel its complexities. Home and family now take on some of the characteristics of the outside world. To our realization, they walk in tandem, one more subtle than the other, but both nefarious to different degrees. Evil comes from ignorance and lack of self-respect. Ignorance nurtures itself with fear and selfishness that strangles freedom. Step by step, the bondage of days gone by loosens its hold, and our new road widens to greet us. Confidence builds in our heart, and our step becomes more swift and sure. We let tomorrow be, for it will soon be today. We let the past go, for it will never be again. We let time die unto itself, and only the present shines its gloriousness, in moments of freedom that never fade away and only become stronger.

WHAT DOES IT MEAN TO BE IN THE FLOW OF LIFE?

What is meant to be stands, ready and waiting for its time to manifest. Any attempt to force life's events meets with fruitlessness and squandering of energy. Life supports us fully when we let go of our foolish notions, settle into our True Self, and drop into the moment. No struggle exists here; it can't. Time does not exist in the moment, so it's impossible to attach to it. If we do not attach, we are in the flow. If we are in the flow, we are living. If we are living, we are truly life. If we are life, we are godlike, because our Father is life. This state brings riches beyond the capacity of our mind to understand. In this state, we are truly free. We are at one with our heavenly Father. We are our Father's children, His blessed children.

HOW IS PEACE FOUND?

We rest and are easy in our own heart, for our true nature lies therein. No need exists for any trepidation or fear to arise. We are assured that we are truly given all we need to address whatever faces us. We let our small voice within calm us and point us to our ever-increasing good. Life continually offers opportunities for us to grow into who we really are. As us face the fears and obstacles that appear to be insurmountable, they simply fall and crumble at our feet. The almighty power of our Father sustains us in all endeavors, and its richness and abundance now pour out into our life. No more must we grovel and fear we will not succeed. No more must we wonder if we are doing the right thing. No more must we doubt our abilities or self-worth. The world opens to us as we open to ourselves. Life comes to those who believe in themselves and their God-given abilities. Success is assured and happiness sings its song in our heart. We let our wings spread as we walk with the dignity that is our True Self. O' Holy Father, we humbly thank You for Your eternal love.

WHAT IS THE ANSWER?

The love of our Father fills us so deeply, and yet we continue to hang onto old ways. The answer is simple. We continue to look to the Light. We rebuke appearances, and instead look within our own heart. We stop pining for better days, because they do not exist. Only in the present moment can our thoughts and feelings give us what we need. So we banish our old ways forever and walked steadily and continually in triumph. There is no need to hurry or capitulate to others' whims. We let them carry their own cross to freedom. A heart and mind that rings with doubt falters and clings to the hell of despair. Only unfaltering commitment and faith can bring us the everlasting freedom of self-acceptance. When we capture the fort of our True Self, the heavens open up to greet us. The arms of our Father are outstretched, waiting for each of His children to come home. O' heavenly Father, give us the strength to carry on to the final destination of the realization of You, manifested through us. Fill us with Your everlasting love and goodness, and let us know we can and must allow ourselves to share our life fully with You.

HOW DO WE MAKE OUR WAY ON THIS ENDLESS JOURNEY?

Distractions come to throw us off and test our resolve. They measure our progress and also teach us our weaknesses. The journey is unending, and this enlightenment gives us pause to simply stop and reflect. We never get there. We *are* there. Life just is. It moves at its own pace; it is up to us to flow with it or fight it. By fighting ourselves, we fight life. The journey goes nowhere, and yet it takes us everywhere.

Realizations calm the mind and set an easiness to the soul. Step after step of awareness continues to lighten the load of ignorance in our heart, and with it, anxiety, frustration, and anger simply dissolve. They aren't real, anyway. They are not us. Life is us, and we are life. Help comes when we make our own way. Ironic, isn't it? Life's paradoxes unfold, and new opportunities for growth open up before us. We do not tire, but instead lift our head. A new adventure awaits us, and as we walk down each new path, we realize more and more the destiny of who we really are. We love our family, cherish our friends, and are kind to our coworkers, but we honor ourselves first, and the righteousness in our life spills out on them as well.

WHAT IS RESPONSIBILITY?

The dawn of life is continual. As our awareness grows, so does our life. The only impairment to realizations is simply ourselves. Every-one's journey must be their own. As a loving spouse, family member, or friend, our duty is to be available to others. However, we are under no obligation to get swallowed up by their self-pity, pain, or unwillingness to take on life's challenges. Life is not structured that way. We are all independent, yet interdependent.

Every person, animal, flower— all living things must act out their own uniqueness and destiny. Responsibility arises in the form of caring without compromising our own well-being. We do no justice to ourselves or for those to whom we are concerned through worry or wanting another's condition to be different. We can listen, nurse, and provide advice when asked. All of us must see our Father's light within ourselves and allow it to shine out with our individual radiance. Only through awareness can anyone realize the fine line between assisting our fellow brothers and sisters through the strength of our independence, or escaping our responsibility through outright selfishness of our own needs. Only by looking deep within our own hearts and asking ourselves our true intentions can we know if we are truly accepting our responsibilities.

WHAT IS TRUE HELP?

We let the anxiety lift from our heart and watch each moment as it unfolds before us. The truth of the matter is we each have set our own path and must follow it. No person has the right to control or manipulate another's destiny. By doing so, they affect their own and bring themselves unhappiness. As each of us follows our small voice and inner promptings, we become stronger and more self-confident. In doing so, we begin to see the failings of our loved ones with more clarity. The anger then subsides; in its place comes frustration and being upset. Although this is progress, it is not the answer. Patience must be exercised, as well as endurance and determination. The mind does not know what to do, but the heart does. We then step back from the frustration, speak with kindness, and say what we feel. We are aware of the others' feelings, however, we never, ever give up our soul. Our Father gave us this most precious gift of eternal life. We ask that our Father guide us through these troubled waters, and by doing so, we help ourselves and the ones we love.

HOW IS THE TRUTH REALIZED?

Heaven graces our brow, as we feel our Father's gentle hand upon our face. The brutality of facing the truth, although drastic in its realizations, does in fact liberate the soul to walk and act more freely. It filters through to the body, which stretches and relaxes in its new comfort. Ah! The harshness of the world forces us to achieve comfort and solace within ourselves. Another of life's paradoxes and mysteries becomes a little more clear today. The veil of deception lies within our own minds. Only through complete faith in the mystery of our Father, and complete trust in His love, can we see life from our soul. Then, we are clear. No veil exists there, because we realize our Father, and our Father is the truth. As we face what we believe is the truth in our minds, we are really facing our fears. As we face our fears, the deceptions dissolve. Then, we see the true picture. We realize our True Self, and the vastness of the universe that lies within us. That vastness is our Father. He expands infinitely and lays out before us treasures that we continually see as we realize more of ourselves.

WHAT DO WE REALLY KNOW?

The simplicity of it all strikes us. This only happens when we settle down within ourselves and trust life. It amazes us, how much we fight the flow. That is from not knowing. We think we don't know, but that is just the a ruse of our mind. In reality, for some reason, we don't want to know. The only world we know is from our own perspective, making it the only world we have. Sometimes people meet—really meet—but most of the time, they sleepwalk by each other in a constant daze. The whole thing is not to rush; there is nowhere to go. We settle down and trust ourselves, and then the world becomes more tender, loving, and filled with infinite possibilities. What a prize our Father has bestowed on us! Immortality with increasing happiness is our inheritance. We let the walls of the fort surrounding our heart and mind come tumbling down; a true fort needs no walls. Then, we are invincible, all-powerful, and in the flow of life itself. This is where our Father exists. All else does not exist. We ask that our eyes be opened, and for our Father to help us see.

HOW IS CLARITY REACHED?

The more we become aware, the clearer we can see the absurdity as well as the blessings. Our mind is so powerful, it dictates our life. So we ask, 'why can't we stop the foolishness right now?' We can. Thought by thought, we change the direction of our life to more peace, more calm, more assurances, more confidence, and more happiness. Can we do that instantaneously? Probably not—the shock would be too great to our mind, and it would probably cause death to our body. So why does it take so long? Maybe it does not. Our progress is swift yet grounded. It's measured not only against this lifetime, but all our lifetimes and eternity itself.

Do we have blessings? Yes, we have abundant blessings of new awareness each and every day. Do we have health? Yes, and we can provide for our spouse, family, and ourselves in comfort. Do we have relatives? Yes, they can provide support for us if we need them. Do we have friends? Yes, true friends who brings us the greatest gift, which is ourselves. Do we have intelligence? Yes, it provides us an unending curiosity to explore more and more. Do we have ourselves? Step by step, we do, and as we acknowledge that, we are gaining the higher ground in our life. As we accept the rewards of our labor, the nonsense of fear, doubts, and insecurity wither away into nothingness. We are blessed with wit, humor, kindness, intelligence, and the will and determination to capture the very essence of our soul. So we see the nonsense fading away. We see our endearing blessings come to us, and our Father brings His prodigal children home.

HOW DOES CHANGE OCCUR?

It seems the fears rise up from within us from nowhere. It is a strong feeling, in that no outside event triggers it as it to shows its ugly face. However, it tells us we are harboring fears and feeding them, so they stay alive within us, deep within us. Why do we do that? What silly nonsense possesses us to hang onto misery, when happiness is our continuous and ultimate goal? The answer seems to be weakness we have not yet rooted out. So how do we become stronger, more alert, stepping fully into the flow of life? What is the answer? We start saying no to those ugly feelings. We start saying yes to this very moment. We stop harboring the past in the form of excuses. We start picturing ourselves as strong, vibrant, and in command of ourselves and our life. We start accepting matters right now in the moment, and choosing to acknowledge confidence, well-being, and happiness, right here where we are. Life gives us every opportunity to choose. We stand up straight, accept ourselves, and we accept others for who they are. They have God-given gifts, and so do we. However, we are all different. It is our privilege to be independent. We can walk alone if we desire, yet we can learn from others, as well teach others. From the legacies we know of great men such as Gandhi, we can free ourselves, and then, by our own example, others can free *themselves*. We stop the madness of our past, which contains all its old fears. We start living right now, in calmness, joy, self-awareness, and self-approval.

HOW IS INSECURITY VANQUISHED?

The tragedy of insecurity puts a mask of deception on life itself. Without remorse or conscience, it robs, plunders, and totally devastates any hope of happiness or joy. False beliefs of outside sources arise in the form of material wealth or acknowledgment of achievements. These are fleeting, and bring yet another desire for more of an unending cycle of want and later disappointment. The treachery the mind walks through cannot be resolved by the intellect alone. The heart must guide the way, as the soul provides the unending power that leads us back to ourselves. Only true awareness of ourselves will free us from the earth's wiles and trickery and set us solidly in happiness. O' heavenly Father, let us see more. We thank You for the angels that we cannot see, who guide us along a our path to freedom. We thank You for sending us who we need along the way, to give us guidance we need in our most dire times. The only way is through You. You are our Father. You are our life. Let us banish the ignorance from our heart and walk with the pride and dignity of who we really are. In kindness and strength, let us lift ourselves up out of the mire of the world. Ignorance breeds insecurity, and insecurity brings helplessness and despair, or arrogance and attack. Let us see even more clearly, and continue to free ourselves to walk in fullness and in the light of Your love.

HOW IS CONDITIONING SEEN?

To see the traits of our life right before our eyes can be a very startling experience. The ugliness of it causes admittance to its truth. So is that really us? Is that really them? We all have uniqueness, and it is that special creation our Father loves so much. He sees yet another aspect of Himself. His children are sprinkled throughout His creation like the stars in the galaxies.

But let's also look at traits. They are not all unique. They do afford insight. They do denote, in a way, conditioning. Conditioning denotes a falseness, since it covers the individual's nature, which is meant to sparkle as a shining star that makes our Father and His universe so grand. So let's accept today our traits, and, in doing so, see through them for what they are. By dropping the conditioning, the world gains clarity and the ultimate gift of freedom. What is freedom? It really cannot be truly defined in words. Words cannot truly express the truth. The truth is beyond words. We can, however, as we gain profound insights into our true nature, become free from prejudice, conflict, worry, and anxiety of what we need to do. A natural flow then comes, which is a uniting of our souls with our Father in a universe that infinitely expands and creates happiness for all those who have the will and determination to see it.

HOW DO WE WORK THROUGH OUR RECURRING PROBLEMS AND WEAKNESSES?

We make our way down our destined path. Even though it tries us, the rewards we receive bring us up short with the amazement of our accomplishments on our road so far. Even though it seems sometimes impossible to resolve a problem or move through overwhelming stress, the light does dawn, and the awareness takes the place of what were once unsurmountable obstacles. Even though triumphs occur, recurring themes in our life come back again and again, to haunt us and force us to face them. Even though we become discouraged at times when we think we have fully resolved a long-standing issue, we must realize we cannot resolve in a day or year what took a lifetime to create.

Our happiness depends on us, even though it would be easy to think otherwise. Our own salvation depends on us, even though we have been taught someone or something else will guide us to the heaven we seek. We ask our heavenly Father for His love, even though we fail sometimes, and trespass against Him and our brothers and sisters. We ask to hear His voice inside us, even though at times we let ourselves get discouraged. We look to see our Father in all things, even though our eyes are not always aware of what truly exists. We want to see the heaven He has in store for us, even though we still walk upon this earth.

WHAT IS THE VALUE OF LESSONS?

Lessons must be learned, and most of the time they cannot be learned right away. It takes patient discipline, laced with ever-unadulterated determination to "Get It." Getting it goes beyond the intellect, right to the soul. The soul must meet up with itself, and the lessons are the vehicle to do that. As each lesson is learned, it seems to instantly vanish and be forgotten as a problem. Just as spontaneously as one lesson is learned, another takes its place. It is in this progress that one must stop to acknowledge the accomplishments of one's own deeds. The right attitude must be set as the next lesson comes into view.

It is not some punishment or burden lain on a weary soul, but instead our Father's helping hand reaching out to grab ours. To trust in His love with complete faith sets the stage for untold, unimaginable rewards and happiness. Self-awareness is the unending goal. Happiness is achieved by accepting where we are right now. Happiness becomes more profound, each time we take our Father's hand as He pulls us forward to more and more realizations of Himself inside us. We need to ponder that. He is within us, around us, and everywhere present. It's a matter of deciding to see Him. We are thankful for our lessons, dear Father.

WHERE IS PEACE?

We actually find it amazing that we continue to yearn for the arrival of peace within ourselves when we are not thankful for what we have right now. It's insane that we know, but still continue in this vein, when we know it's fruitless. This is a sad way to live. Instead, the way is to just relax. We simply need to take a moment and look at yesterday, last week, last month, and last year. Life is very good. We are happier, more settled, and most definitely more aware of who we are and how the world really works. Yes, what a great realization, to just settle down into the goodness within ourselves and feel the calm we keep running after. Oh yes, we let it come. We cannot chase it down and capture what we already have. We settle down. We simply settle down. We do have pearls and gold that have value beyond our wildest dreams. Oh! We just let it come. We are thankful, humble, and, most of all, aware. As wasteful thoughts take flight, we see the light. O' Father, there You are. We didn't need to go so far.

HOW ARE WE SHOWN THE LIGHT?

Today was a good day. We fared well with our new realizations, which keep coming as our own light becomes brighter and shows through. We are becoming alive and aware of a new existence, an existence we are meant to see clearly and unencumbered. The raw truth of the traumas in our life come roaring in like a violent storm that hits the coast in the winter months. The wind comes with such force, it blows the top off a lifetime illusion of a lie that kept us buried in doubt, anxiety, and a continual wandering for the truth, which we knew existed deep in our heart. From that darkness, which so covered our life, we now see the light of day, as its glimmer begins to touch the green leaves of the trees once again. We, step by step, walk out of the deceit and illusion into the glory of who we really are.

The light is there, if we so desire to see it. It cannot be denied, because it just is. It waits patiently for us to see it. Tragedy befalls us for one purpose, so we will triumph. In triumph, we live, and, in living, we love. In loving, we are *indestructible*. As we proclaim our power within us, weakness leaves us, the wounds of deep hurt heal, and our Father, in all His goodness, opens his arms to us and bestows such untold gifts that we must bow our head and bend our knee to Him. In thanksgiving, we now accept the Light.

WHAT IS OUR CHOICE?

The jeopardy we live under in this world is extremely high, if we really look at the stakes. It is our Father or nothing. There is no compromise, and the road is treacherous and tough. It is all relative. Of course, it is. We don't have it as bad as those who live in dire poverty in a third-world country, or those who wake up to an inner city's cruelty every day. However, the challenges we face are our own, and they are there to make us realize who we really are. If we meet life head-on, life will respond with gifts of such magnitude that any words will pale in their presence. Our thoughts lead the way to our success. If we cannot control them, we will wander in a wasteland of doubt and ineptitude. We will get turned around by the world, every time it takes a breath.

To be the master of our soul takes a colossal, concerted effort with no compromise. To look at the daunting task in its entirety is foolish, but to proceed faithfully, one step at a time, leads to a multitude of victories that make the pain of each step be forgotten in an instant. Just one more thing, just one more thing, and we will be happy. This is fallacy. It doesn't matter where we are on our journey. It just matters that we are on it. Most never start out on their road. They hide in many façades and beliefs that close them down and leave them in the unhappiness of false hopes and dreams never truly fulfilled.

The call comes from deep inside our soul. To ignore it spells disaster and a wasted life. After the kids have grown and left, after the career and the retirement parties are over, after the money is saved and the house is paid for, we realize what we really have. Of course, mistakes were made, and really, that is the best part of our lives, if we have learned from them, accepted ourselves, and moved on. However, if we are stuck in old memories and "should have's," we are not living in the light of our Father's presence. Instead, we live in a dark shadow of wanting, and, most probably, self-pity.

So, today, we must take stock and decide where we want to be on the road to the realization of ourselves, with ever-increasing happiness, or stuck in a barrage of false hopes, sadness, and emptiness that aches and causes untold turmoil. We turn to our Father. He is always there for us.

WHAT DOES ACCEPTING LIFE MEAN?

To just relax and soak it in is the goal. This statement sets off all kind of alarms inside us, of how we are going to be able to do that. What a senseless struggle we put ourselves through. Yet we stand in this ignorance, hanging on tightly to fears, are so familiar to us that we invite them to stay, and even ask them if they would like a cup of tea and a biscuit. Urges come from within us to complain and feel sorry for ourselves, and they are strong. They have had a lot of practice, and hold on tenaciously, not to be dissolved. Our life has taken on a new perspective, however, and the clarity of that new perspective comes more and more each day. We find the knots of entanglement loosen, even though they have not yet been untied. Our blessings are becoming more apparent. Life does become calmer, easier, and smoother. We open ourselves to the flow of life, with its tumultuous as well as peaceful times. A flat surface is restful after a roaring river's current of waves, but sitting stagnant or moving slowly causes boredom and stagnation. So we must make our choice now, to live the way we have been, or to move more freely into a new life. It may look the same from the outside, but from the inside it has a whole new feel. We transform our mind and open ourselves to the abundant riches of life and the goodness that is ourselves.

WHAT ARE OUR CHOICES?

The mysteries of life must be accepted; otherwise, we can never be happy. Life unfolds into infinity, and unless we come to terms with that, we will always be upset, fearful, and "on the run." There is nowhere to go but here and now. Thought patterns dictate our perceptions and therefore our reality. Our life seems like it is the same as it has always been, but when we look in the mirror, we see a happier person, who is now more mature and more accepting. We also see a person with many faults. We are extremely fortunate and blessed to be able to wipe away the mire in our life and see the reality more truly every day.

First, there is a new awareness, then an observation, and finally an acceptance. It is from the point of acceptance that we must make our choice. Do we say 'okay, we will live with it,' or know it will just not do? Sometimes, the choices are easy; other times, the pain is excruciating. How do we decide? We must be true to our own nature and disposition, and never, ever waiver. Yes, it is much easier said than done, but it is the only way for us to unburden ourselves from the unnecessary, and sometimes outright silly, circumstances we find ourselves faced with. We cannot be rude, and we cannot be timid. We cannot blame our past, but we can become aware of it, and by doing so, finally free ourselves from its grip. So we discard what is no longer needed. If we don't know what to do, we wait. We simply pray, and the answer comes. Then, another new dawn shines on our life, and our happiness becomes even more.

HOW IS A LIGHTER LIFE ACHIEVED?

We awaken to another day, as we see the sun rising to meet us. All that occurred yesterday is now the past, and we can let go of it. People are the way they are; we have no power over them, nor do we want it. So, by the same reasoning, they have no power over us. That means we can control our own emotions and feelings, regardless of others' words or actions. It is the conditioning of our own thoughts and feelings that make us react in the same old way, with the same old patterns. With this realization, it gives the appearance that it would be so easy to change course into a more fulfilling, joyful life.

Yet we watch ourselves, as our reactions to the same events occur again and again. Instead, we see now that we have a choice. We can grow past these detrimental feelings, thoughts, and emotions into a lighter existence, one that brings more laughter, more flow, and more enjoyment to our life. How do we accept our current state? How do we accept others' faults and live with them? How do we accept our own faults and learn to love ourselves? These are good questions, but what are the answers? We just let things go, and don't take them so seriously. Life goes on, no matter how we think or feel. So we need to face the facts of life, which at sometimes can be very cruel, and move on, just move on.

HOW ARE WE FREED BY AWARENESS?

As our awareness expands, it sets a clear picture of the world we see before us. The characters in this play take on a less mysterious and confusing role. We see their true motives, attitudes, and intelligence with more objectivity, and that releases us from nagging burdens. Pretty much the same results occur, but we find we are not as wrapped up in the outcomes. It is a downright absurd existence, to view the world through the eyes of ignorance. As we become more aware, the fear falls off, and it leaves us more relaxed and peaceful. The task is not easy, be assured, but the rewards are beyond words.

The funny thing is, we cannot run around telling everyone about it. That act would just dissolve our victories. The Kingdom of our Father is truly within us, and that relationship is only between us and our Father. It is subjective; there is no slide rule anyone can pull out to measure happiness or peace. That does not matter. There is no competition involved, and no conspiracy can exist to assert our position. We are just who we are, and the realization of ourselves clarifies our outer world and sets us loose to move more freely in it. We drop the false illusions. We face the truth and walk free.

HOW ARE ILLUSIONS HANDLED?

We say, 'Begone, all you nasty, unproductive thoughts. In your place, may positiveness and confidence rise up in triumph and establish peace.' May we become comfortable with the uncomfortable and believe in ourselves to ride the waves and currents of life as they come to meet us. To live with the paradoxes of life opens the door to life through acceptance. Integrity and truth hold the only reality, and therefore are all we really have to hold on to. There is nothing else. All else is transitory. So we let the big bogeyman of illusions jump and scream, even treating him to an ice cream cone if he wants it. We just can't sit down with him at his table. We must keep allowing the truth that waits in our soul to be manifest through us. We keep a light and joyful heart, and a positiveness to our disposition, never surrendering to guilt, shame, anxiety, or doubts. They are cover ups; in a feeble way, they try to kill the soul. Our soul always has existed and always will exist. We simply vow to enjoy ourselves. It's our Father's will and our heritage. Our Father loves us, and His angels protect us from any harm.

HOW IS LIFE TRULY ENJOYED?

Our journey takes its twists and turns through unknown territories. We become more at peace, and our mind becomes more relaxed, as we take on a lighter tone. Even though we are becoming more aware, the harsh stick of reality pokes us in the eye and sets us back on our duff. As we lie there in pain, we also find a relief in knowing the truth about the ugliness of life. There is no magic pill or shortcut, and, if anybody espouses their wares as such, be aware. Life is filled with traps, and we can get stuck, if we are not true to ourselves. In addition, the angels stand ready against any harm that might befall us. We have been taught to 'transform your mind,' but the task resounds in monumental proportion. There is no need to get discouraged, though. It's a step-by-step proposition, so we enjoy the walk on our journey, for each moment we experience will never come again. We enjoy the pilgrimage of our soul awakening to itself and lavish in the failures as well as the triumphs. It's all good, really; it shows us our true nature. We are all vibrant and resilient, with an infinite capacity to overcome any obstacle on the road to ever-increasing, well-earned happiness.

HOW CAN WE PROGRESS AND MOVE FORWARD?

Although our intelligence can be keen and our view of how the world works clear, our happiness will never occur, unless we fully accept the Father within ourselves. To do that, we must first accept ourselves with all our many flaws. It is easy to look outward, but very, very difficult to look within. There, we will find the pain we need to heal and let go. Once we start on our journey, it never ends. So we need to just start, and the happiness we so desperately seek, we will start to realize. The other alternative is to be stuck in the sticky muck we have built up in our mind, some of which we might not even be aware of.

Life is an opportunity that cannot be wasted. It offers a way to happiness and freedom. We must take it, or else we will be spinning our wheels and standing still in the same place in our life, wondering why. We can blame ourselves or someone else, but we will still be stuck. So we move our attention within, and, automatically, our life will begin to transform into more happiness and love. We muster up the courage to start our journey. The angels protect us along the way. We have faith our way will be lit before us. We have hope, and it fuels our progress. We have love of our Father and ourselves, and it brings us untold peace and happiness. To become unstuck, we start our journey home right now.

WHAT IS THE WAY TO HAPPINESS?

It's a mishmash of incoherent and irrelevant thoughts that cause confusion and inaction. It is leftover stinky mental garbage we have hauled around from our early childhood. As we become more aware and move through the muck, we see more and more of the unnecessariness of it. It is wrong thinking that causes distrust, unfounded results, and unhappiness. The game in this world is a monster of immense proportion; as our awareness grows, we keep realizing a higher stakes game we are playing. The gist of it is to "hang tough" with the belief in ourselves, and to exercise faith in our Father's unending love and nurturing of our soul.

What athlete or great concert pianist has achieved much without dedication, determination, and a whole lot of practice? The same goes for the game on the stage of life. Absolute surrender is necessary to our Father's will, with unending faith. Then, He is with us. That is the way to ever-increasing happiness. Perfection, then, is an illusion. The process of creation is life itself. It never stands still. It is always moving toward more fulfillment through change, and we must do the same. Our direction must not come from what we read in books, but instead from what comes from our heart. We do not fear the worst, but instead have faith to do our best, and in doing so, we will bless ourselves, our loved ones, our family and friends, and, most of all, our Father, who is our source. Our Father wants to be happy too.

HOW ARE DISAGREEMENTS HANDLED?

There is nothing wrong with listening to other people's opinions. We can take them into consideration and see if their ideas fit for us, or if we see things differently. Even though we might not agree with them, we don't have to feel angry or bad about it. They have a right to think what they want to think, and so do we. Open, honest discussion is healthy, but we don't have to agree with each other. We can also listen to someone else's perspectives about us, weigh it and accept some or part of it, or just discard it. That is up to us. There is no absolute right or wrong answer. There are just different perspectives. We must remember two important things, however. We must be true to ourselves. If it does not feel right to us, it just plain is not. If we find we truly have been fooling ourselves and someone has hit a nerve with what they said, we must fess up to ourselves. We can fess up to them only if we want to. Next, we must respect the other person for their point of view. They have a right to it, even though we don't like it. If they are obnoxious about it, there is no need to take their guff. In that way, we respect ourselves, and awareness keeps coming. We just need to be patient and enjoy the ride.

HOW IS TRUE MEANING FOUND?

The light from the morning sun filters through the window and signals the start of a new day. Our thoughts stir, as we experience a glimmer of realization. We know we have the power to control them. As with anything, a new endeavor might feel daunting and highly improbable to complete, but, of course, that is not the case. Our experience shows, time and time again, we overcome what is laid out before us. The will is extremely powerful, a mighty sword on this journey. It literally cuts through the bindings of our life, sometimes with great force, and other times with the gentleness of a small child. Our Father grants us our every desire, as He reflects back to us our own thoughts from His infinite awareness. To buttress the gift of will, our Father grants us faith, determination, hope, and patience. Armed with these virtues, the world bends to our every desire and grants us our most sought-after longings. We must remember, though, our success lies only within us. When we honor our true nature and drop the false thinking acquired in our childhood—learned from well-meaning but ignorant parents and teachers—we accomplish much, and, most of all, are happy and fulfilled with our results. It's all up to us; no one can possibly make our decisions for us. We pray often for the right answers to come from within us, and we move quickly to act on our promptings. They are right for us and bring the freedom of peace our Father so desires for us.

HOW CAN FAITH BE USED?

We feel a sense of going crazy as we become more aware of our circumstances, but we know we are not. It's amazing to have lived one way so long; the unnaturalness of it seems so normal. As we awaken, we cringe at the way we have lived and the way we are living now. We doubt and wonder how we will be able to undo the bindings of our life and live with laughter and spontaneity. At the same time, we feel a sense of faith and confidence that our Father hears our prayers and will see us through. With faith and guidance, we can overcome any obstacles. We have faced and conquered many to reach this point in our life, and, with determination and faith, we will overcome what lies on our path to free our soul. The subtleties and non-overtness of the way we live pull at our heart and bring us signs of impossibilities, but that is just an illusion. The answer is to pray and grow in faith; in that way, our Father's love grants us the awareness we need to see ourselves through. As the picture becomes more clear, it becomes more ugly, but it's only through the truth that we free ourselves. O' Heavenly Father, hear our prayer and let us stand with confidence and faith as we heal ourselves.

WHAT DO WE SEE WITHIN US AND BEFORE US?

Today, we admit a weakness of constant fear. It hangs around our neck like a giant stone, weighing us down and blocking us from looking straight ahead into our new life. Hallelujah! We just said it. It is time to pull it out by its roots and throw it away. All things are possible; as we practice optimism and believe—truly believe—in our own innate nature of strength, we know our success is assured. As we take a new direction, heaven is assured. Life is a blessing. Smiles and laughter can come freely. Happiness can be sustainable. Awareness can expand. Calmness and peace can be permanent. Health can be established and sustained. Financial resources can be plenty. Families can reunite. Marriages can be happy and flowing. Reality can be realized, and truth can be known. All our Father's gifts can be received. Happiness can be ours.

WHAT IS TRUE ACHIEVEMENT?

We make our way through life really on our own. Our parents, family, and teachers guide us and mold us into what they think we should be. Most of the time, their intentions are good—sometimes not, but all in all, we still have to find our own way through life, from the bully in the schoolyard to the boss we just can't stand. There is a bright side to this, as we discover our talents and creativity. Joy rings in our heart, because what we are doing is fun and builds self-confidence and the awareness of who we truly are. As we look back at our life—really look—we can see the framework and structure, and how we came to where we are today. There is no need for sorrow, blame, or regrets. It brings instead renewal and celebration. We really have accomplished much under very severe circumstances. We keep that in our mind and hold it there. That is our beacon of light that shines for ourselves and others to see. Now, as life washes away our footprints in the sand of our earthly achievements, we need to remember what we left in the hearts and minds of those who were able to touch us and whom we touched. This is what lasts forever.

WHAT CHOICES NEED TO BE MADE?

It's funny, how fear creeps into our mind and simply wants to stay there. There is always a choice, and, once a choice is made, it eventually turns into a pattern. It's okay to fail, if we learn from it. The point is that we try and try again, and don't take any of it to heart. We know who we are and what we can do. As we look deeper and deeper into our soul, the magnitude of possibilities available brings an inner peace. Unique talents abide in all of us. With humility, as we honor them, life smooths out and settles down. There is no easy or free ride; that is for sure. However, the realization and acceptance of ourselves light up the world to our beck and call. Through hard work and determination, this supports us at every turn. Life unfolds in a right rhythm. The truth revealed allows souls to reach out to each other with true companionship and honor. We stop the madness in our mind of failure and worry. There is no failure. There is always just another step to success. The success of peace, happiness, and fulfillment waits for those who dare to honor the talents and gifts our Father bestows upon us. We move on. We keep going and pick up our speed to take flight, soar on the winds of change, and look from on high at our accomplishments.

HOW ARE THE THOUGHTS IN OUR MIND CONTROLLED?

The realizations pour into our mind, as it becomes more porous, allowing the light to come in. Desperately, the old ways hang on as they fail at every step and become still weaker. Wishful thinking thumbs its nose at us; as we learn the gift of acceptance, we now stand the test of what seems so impossible before us. Our Father's will knows no boundaries, and offers sincerity and help for all those who surrender to it. As we realize our successes, we stand back in wonderment at the gifts we have and the blessings our Father bestows on us. If we surrender, we are good. If we struggle, we remain in turmoil. Our physical illnesses tell the story, when we struggle with conflicting thoughts, pessimistic thinking, and lack of self-confidence.

We can succeed. Our life's experiences as small children and young men and women have taught us that. To doubt ourselves is silly and foolish. If we buy into other people's sickness and foolishness, we have bought into our own weaknesses. Awareness is the answer, and awareness can only be gained through sincerity, honesty, and pure determination. Realizations only come because we want them to come. Wishful thinking is detrimental to achieving awareness, because awareness brings reality, which is the truth. If we stop thinking negative thoughts, all that is left is happiness. As we accept what's before us, we realize with clarity what we can change and what is out of our control in our life. In that way, we stop struggling. We stop letting people get us down. We have control over this. We look at the source. Ignorance has no power over the truth. We lighten our load of worrisome thoughts. We let our mind be open to our Father's direction, and life beckons to us true happiness.

WHAT IS THE MOST IMPORTANT DECISION WE NEED TO MAKE?

We stop fearing the unknown and welcome it. It offers infinite possibilities, and, with that, infinite successes. We need to take the long road. Yes, we turn over every rock, stone, and pebble. We honor our true nature, and it honors us. Our Father forgives us, so we must forgive ourselves. Perfection in this world is an illusion the ego strives to sustain; however, truth offers room for continual growth and ever-increasing happiness. Our Father never lets us down. Only we let ourselves down.

We need to be kind to ourselves in all circumstances, and in that way, our pain is eased and our success is tempered with humility. True happiness can only be gained by complete surrender to our Father. We must always, always ask Him for help and direction. In that way, success is assured. We make sure of what we want, and then we make up our mind to get it. As difficulties come, we are thankful; they are stretching and molding our soul, so we can realize even more happiness. We never despair or harbor self-pity; that gives away our power. We use our talents to buoy ourselves and help others. We lose ourselves in the work our Father lays before us, and as we do, a joy settles into our arms and then drops tenderly into our lap. Heaven waits until we are ready to accept it, as we realize who we really are. Otherwise, we will wander and search for a happiness that does not exist. We turn our mind and heart over to our Father and settle into the flow of life. The decision is up to us.

WHAT IS LIFE?

We slow down and really see what's going on. The reality is all around us. Our perceptions make our reality. Life is a grand gift of opportunities for learning, growth, and self-fulfillment. Only we can accept its challenges, and, by doing so, redeem ourselves from our own insecurities and lack of faith. Whatever befalls us is really our own creation. Rather, let's say what we let befall us is our own creation—that is better. Lack of faith and maturity causes the problems. We have to be strong, very strong. No easy answers exist; why should they? How else do we learn and therefore understand?

Most people don't care, because they are too self-absorbed with their own agenda and ambition of grandeur. It's a pity, but that's how it is. It's only through faith and self-determination that we can lift ourselves up. It takes a lot of patience; this is not an overnight process. If we change our mind to be positive and throw away all of our lacking and negative thoughts, our world *must* get better. In that way, we provide for ourselves the opportunity to use our talents to express ourselves. That's all we really want to do, anyway. Life is a gift, and it's ours to do with whatever we want. We cleanse our mind of the refuse of despair, fear, and lack of faith. We step into the positive realm of achievement and self-fulfillment. We meet each challenge with a smile. We use the gifts our Father gave us with humility, and thank our Father for the gift of life.

HOW IS FAITH STRENGTHENED?

There is a nasty element that can take over our thinking, and it does so with a cocky smile. Awareness, again, is the answer. It's awareness, along with prayer, that provides the solution. Both point to our Father. Yes, we have walked out of the Garden of Eden into a desert of ignorance, self-gratification, and self-pity. So we need to find our way back to the heritage of happiness that is ours. We must be alert to what is around us and dispel negative thinking. A positive outlook generates positive results. We must keep telling ourselves that, with true belief and complete self-confidence. It is required to be strong with our thinking. We put our loved ones into the hands of our Father; that will strengthen our faith. Faith brings comfort itself against all outward appearances. We settle down and let appearances go. Just doing so brings a restful peace to us and those for whom we care. We have no power to change anyone. So we let them go to use their own God-given capabilities; they will find their own way. Our Father waits for all of us to come to Him for His help in complete faith. We need to finally just let go.

HOW ARE DECISIONS MADE?

There is no other way through it than with our Father. The circumstances of life slap us in the face and then walk away, flaunting their triumph. Life is set before us to strengthen us and make us more aware. When we transform our mind with faith and confidence, true solutions come. They do, if we let them. Our Father never abandons us. It is we who make the choice to abandon Him. With that, He still forgives us, each and every time we make that decision. The gift of free will gives us unlimited power. It is what we decide to do with it that is of the utmost importance. We must be true to our own nature, and never give up our soul. Our soul is our most precious gift. It is our Father Himself. We allow ourselves to relax and listen to our own heart. We are kind, compassionate, and, above all, aware. We are aware of who we truly are. We hold to our faith and march confidently through life. We take life one step at a time, and cherish each moment as it comes. We honor ourselves and our loved ones. We are very strong in our faith. Then, and only then, can we swing the world by its tail. Our Father's blessings await us.

HOW IS OPTIMISM ACHIEVED?

The reality is that only our Father can enlighten our mind. We just need to be willing to let Him. There must be an absolute, full-fledged decision to allow our Father to take charge. Joy only comes through complete surrender. The hawk in our mind can only take flight if we let go of the weight of wasteful thoughts so our Father can fill the wings of our mind with such force to lift us out of mundane misery into a world of promise, calm, and peace with Him. Anything is possible, and evidence exists that, time and time again, those who commit themselves to spiritual principles and unending faith in our Father achieve their dreams and walk happy upon this earth. It is required that we really look at ourselves and be aware of the very fine subtleties and patterns of our thinking; then, we will see the truth. Positivity brings happy results. Pessimism and negative thinking bring boredom, uncertainty, and, if we are not careful, outright misery and destruction. No, we don't put our head in the sand and take a Pollyanna outlook. Instead, we are aware and realistic. We take our Father's hand and lift our mind to unbelievable heights of the joy and happiness that come with optimism. That is a gift from our most loving and Almighty Father.

WHAT CAN BE FOUND IN EACH MOMENT?

We let our Father's Spirit glow, and with each thought and step, we let our life become brighter. We are so special and dear to our Father, and He loves us so much. His every thought and breath is for our happiness. We are His children; if we could only taste a slight drop of His love, it would overpower us on this earthly plane. What treasures we possess, and what gifts we are granted to use here on earth! We stop hiding and come out of ourselves. We greet the world head-on, with a great big smile of who we really are. There is no time to waste. It is so precious; each moment is eternity itself. It is truly in eternity where we live. Yes, there is no yesterday and there is no tomorrow.

There is just now, in this moment. Therefore, each moment is blessed, sacred, and a gift. We stand up straight and are confident as we seize the moment and flow with our God-given goodness; that's all that really exists. We reach deep inside ourselves and realize the heaven that lies within our soul. We are thankful and humble and feel blessed. We open our heart fully to our Father, who loves us with His almighty strength, and we feel the joy of our eternal connection to our Heavenly Father. All is good. All is our Father.

WHAT MAY WE ASK OF OUR FATHER?

The road seems so long, but it brings riches we could never have dreamed possible. Our life now lights up with hope, and a soothing peace brings us rest as we learn to allow it. It's all up to us; it always has been. Our awareness grows, and our strength builds. We are in a land now that once was so very far away. The answer lies in our Father and the trust we put in Him. He is supporting our every step, and granting us peace whenever we ask. We are tested; our faith is tried. It's only through true belief in our Father and ourselves that we succeed.

What happiness we feel in this thought! We are never alone; we are never abandoned. Our Father is always with us. We are always forgiven, and we are encouraged with words of wisdom, kindness, and comfort. Our Father lets us enjoy what we have achieved, and gives us the strength to see more of life and the mysteries of its blessings. We ask for His help for us to keep a true heart and walk with the dignity of our true Spirit. We ask for help to remove the temptations from our mind, and instead reach deeper into who we really are. We ask for the strength to truly love Him. We ask Him to light up our mind, so we can see and hear His voice clearly. We ask for help to be more thankful to Him. We ask Him to let us drop our arrogance, so we may truly do His will. It is only with Him that we can truly be happy and completely whole. Our life has changed, and this has only been possible because He has sent us the help we need. We ask that our heavenly Father hear our prayer, keep us from temptation, and allow our soul to be filled with His love.

HOW IS OUR FATHER'S PRESENCE KNOWN TO US?

It comes in and out like an ebb and flow. First, it's feelings of unsurmountable stress and impossibilities, and then a tranquil calm sets in that rests our soul. It is called faith; with it, we literally hang on for dear life. Our Father is always with us. It's just that, sometimes, we don't believe it. As we keep our mind focused on our Father, our success is assured. As we pray to Him, He rights our mind and imparts His truth upon us. It is heaven. He stands in heaven and waits for us. He watches us with love, and He is proud of His children. He sends angels to stand at our side to keep us from harm. He eases our mind, when we let Him. He fill us with love, when we open ourselves to Him. He is with us, day and night, into eternity. We can go nowhere without Him. He is part of us, and we are part of Him. The unity of our soul with Him binds us forever in eternal happiness. We must throw off the trappings of the world and the falsehoods of our mind. Then, and only then, will we see Him. He waits for our return.

WHAT IS THE ROLE OF OUR TALENTS?

It grips us and won't let us go. It's part of us, and its discovery from inside ourselves gives us relief, joy, and wonder. We feel like an instrument being played, a play acted out, or a dance that brings so much pleasure with its beauty and grace. We cannot deny ourselves and our talents; by neglecting or hiding them, we sell our soul. We cannot even breathe. Release of creativity is but an act of our Father's expression through our soul, acknowledged in our heart, conceived in our mind, and expressed in the physical world. It is a gift that must be shared, and it grows through that very act. The world thirsts for creativity, originality, and the freedom of expression. Fear, control, and manipulation keep true expression suppressed, so it never sees the light of itself. In very rare instances, it breaks through, and the glory of our Father's gifts shine so bright, it calls attention to itself because of its beauty and truth. The world aches for justice, mercy, and answers; it lives in such a negative environment of hopes never fulfilled, unending struggle, and a continual sense of wandering.

Our Father sends out beacons of light to enrich men's souls, to lift them out of their everyday trials and give them hope and courage so they can accomplish their dreams. There are no magic formulas. True expression comes from total love of our Father, and an awareness of our true nature, which is really Him. It is all Him. He shares Himself freely with us, and we, being Him, must freely express ourselves with others. We must be bold with our talents, and let them rise to meet the negativity and ridicule of the world. The world cannot stand to see the truth, but righteous souls wander and thirst for the truth. We allow them our Father's expression, and by doing so, we acknowledge our True Self, which is our Father in us.

HOW IS THE TRUTH CHOSEN?

There is a choice. There is always a choice. We can choose the truth, or not choose the truth. If we go after our personal endeavors with hopes of happiness, we are running after our own tail. It's an unending cycle of another endeavor of un-fulfillment. Why do we feel lost? Why do we feel sorrow? Why do we get angry? Why do we cry when we don't have the answers? Why do we blame others? Why do we make excuses? Why do we look for security in the world, when there is none? When we seek the truth, we truly live. When we seek anything else, we die. When we give up our desires, we begin to live. We see each moment for what it is, and we truly live it. We don't try to manipulate it. We don't wish the circumstances were different. We don't turn it off with distractions. We experience it head-on for what it is. We accept it, enjoy it, and move on to the next moment. Truth is brutal, but it's all we have. We take on the rough times, and let them mold our soul. We enjoy the tender times; they are the sustenance to see us through the hard times. Our Father's love for us is so rich and full, He gives us our own special talents and the opportunity to use them. We accept the truth. Hard times are opportunities to break down the walls of deception and see the truth more clearly. We choose the truth.

WHAT STEPS MUST WE TAKE?

Another dawn lights up the sky, and a new day begins, but it's different today than yesterday. There is a little more bounce in our step. There is a little more love swelling in our heart. There is a little more clarity in our mind. There is a little more strength in our soul. Wondrous indeed is the mightiness of our Father; through His love, he bestows on us the same mightiness and boldness. This is the training ground of our Father's love. It teaches us our Father's mercy and tenderness. It teaches us our own strength. It teaches us millions and millions of football fields of patience. It teaches us of the most precious gift of who we really are.

We are splendid pearls and diamonds of our Father Himself. We are strewn across the universe in a magnificent display, like the stars that so gloriously decorate the sky. We hold up our heads in the realization of our heritage from our Father. His mighty force of love and courage swells up in us as we allow it. So little by little, every day, every hour, and every minute, we surrender to our Father. We let him fill us up. We open our soul ever wider and wider, that we may be filled overflowing with His tender and compassionate love. We realize who we really are. We accept our responsibility and our heritage. We give into each moment and lay ourselves out before Him. We surrender our life to Him. We love Him more and more. Then, we will know His glory. Then, we will truly be as One. Then, we will truly, truly be happy and at peace. The world will be clear to us, because we have accepted and loved ourselves. All will be aright with us. We take the plunge.

HOW IS OUR FATHER'S PROMISE FULFILLED?

It's amazing, to view life with more clarity. It lightens a load within ourselves, in which we had carried others. Other people's disgruntled, negative, condescending, or sarcastic behavior was pure poison to us, as we took it on in the form of anger, frustration, and fear, accompanied by unending feelings of anxiety and helplessness. The clarity the truth brings us breaks down these feelings. Our strength builds, and our outlook brightens. It is true. We have no need to conquer or vanquish another, nor discredit their intentions. We have no need to argue, belittle, or disagree with anyone. We have no need to get the upper hand. Instead, the clarity brings us the truth about ourselves. We are intelligent, strong, kind, compassionate, honest, and truthful.

As we stand with our Father, our Father stands with us. The negative, piercing arrows no longer sting as much. The essence of our Spirit becomes more manifest. Our confidence builds. We stand taller, and life greets us with a more positive influence. Why? We have given it more of our strength, love, and understanding. It is true: as we give, we do receive. Eventually, negative influences can no longer affect or vanquish us. As we progress on our path to our Father, we become more positive and wear the shield of His Holiness, which protects us from the trickery and wiles of the world. The world cannot see beyond itself, so it is limited. As we engulf ourselves in our Father's love and power, we walk with more ease and calmness within that power.

We have power not over anyone else. We simply have power and control over ourselves. We think and act in accord to our True Self, to our godly nature. The strain has fallen away, and life fills us completely, as we risk it all for our Father. We love Him above our spouse, family, friends, career, car, clothes, and any of our desires.

Our Father waits for us. In return for our love, our Father grants us His. This is the covenant between our Father and His children.

HOW DOES CLARITY COME?

As the shackles fall from our mind, we gain more clarity. The overbearing heaviness recedes, and an easiness and naturalness begin to set in. The anger and frustration are losing their battle, although they fight on with great ferocity and tenacity. The negativity of the outside world becomes more and more apparent and clear. The ignorance that accompanies it now shows its face, more and more every day. The world just is that way; acceptance of it brings happiness, even in the midst of its vicious tactics. However, as we see life's game, we build up a confidence to master it. How is that possible? We just work on ourselves. That's what we truly have control over. With faith in our Father, all things are possible. Yes, mountains can be moved, and the rich happiness our Father holds for us flows into our soul; we are nourished by it. We must be humble and thankful. Without being so, we will once again be tossed around in the world's treachery, like a leaf on a windy autumn day. Our faith must be great, or else we will walk alone.

WHAT IS THE WAY TO TRUE EXISTENCE?

Heaven blesses us and gives us calm. The world keeps milling around us with all its discourtesy, ignorance, and outright foolishness, and yet a detachment is occurring. Through awareness and strength, we take our place as our Father's child. His vastness fills us as we allow it. We must humble ourselves and have faith; only then are we made aright. Negativity can have no power over us unless we let it. Everyone and everything must rise to who they really are. Divinity is our heritage and gift. Pure, unadulterated love exists in us; that is who we really are. The madness exists within our own minds, because we choose it.

What are the options? It's madness or our Father. He needs us, and we need Him. We surrender our heart and mind to Him, and all is right, good, whole, and blessed. What a destiny it is to be His child eternally! What richness that thought inspires. Blessed be His name and the angels who sing His praise. Blessed are we, His children, who now stand with Him at His side. All else is nothing. We ask You, O' Heavenly Father, to fill our soul, to give us strength and show us what it is You want us to do. Let us see our happiness. Father, hear our prayer. Let us see Your way for us. That is our path and our true existence.

WHAT IS VICTORIOUS LIVING?

As we become more aware, we see more insanity. As the anger arises from inside us, we see more sense in letting it go; before, we hung onto it tightly. Before, we asked: why are they like that? Why are they doing this to us? How can they be so stupid? Why don't they care? They are so selfish and insensitive. Our awareness is bringing us through that thinking. It allows us to detach more. We must remember that the process is very slow and painful at times, but we do see our progress. That gives rise to hope and optimism. Instead of trying to escape these trials, we face them with more maturity, and, in any given incident or moment, we are more aware of how we feel. Sometimes we handle it well; sometimes we don't, but we are learning. We see on TV or read about how other people have handled their lives, and that gives us hope. If they have been successful as human beings, why can't we be successful? Determination, coupled with love, spells victory.

It sounds glamorous, now, doesn't it? It's not. It's very hard work, but it is worth it. It brings peace, contentment, and—most of all— happiness. We *can* handle life, with all its trickery, evil, negativity, and trials. We can stretch our heart and soul, and they will not break. We can open our mind and see new things. It's only through awareness and our Father's love that we can experience true happiness.

Blessed are those that listen—really listen—to our Father, and pray to Him in earnest and with regularity. We cannot do it on our own. That is simply foolishness. We let our Father take over. That is the only way.

WHAT IS AWAKENING?

The blistering madness gives way to peace, as courage fills our life and it becomes easier. It is faith that soothes our soul and calms us. It is clarity of our mind that shows us the true landscape of life, and it is our Father who shows us how to handle it. We have looked to distractions for escape, spending time foolishly on wishful thinking. Both of these bring us nothing but frustration and a nagging sense of not being fulfilled. Lately, we feel more at ease with who we are. We are meant to be ourselves. Our intellect and true nature are great gifts that, if used wisely, bring us much happiness, wealth, and success. We shunned our gifts before with feelings of inadequacy. O' what riches we possess! We have a keen mind accompanied by deep insights and sensitivity. Our path is made clear and open. The road now smooths out. There are still hills to climb and bends in the road, but we are now armed with the awareness of who we are. Our self-discovery stirs in us an optimism. What a glorious life we now see, filled with hope and the promise of true blessings, brought about by hard work, determination and faith in the love of our Father. Truly, as we seek, we find; as we knock, the door is open to us. This arduous path makes us stronger, more resilient, and in charge of ourselves. O' heavenly Father, fill our soul. Give us strength and show us what we need to do. Let us see our happiness.

WHAT IS THE USE OF FAILURES?

Although the depth of our soul aches for answers, we must wait patiently for them to come. Our Father will not deny us, and we will not deny ourselves. We failed yesterday. We allowed the imperfections of the world to overwhelm and take over our mind, emotions, and body. We saw the stark madness of the world yesterday, and it upset us. We saw the insanity of people, and it upset us. We saw ourselves against the backdrop of the world, and it upset us. Should we say we allowed it to upset us? Yes, that is more accurate. It showed us our own imperfections, and undoubtedly we did not want to accept that; if we did, it would not have caused us such upheaval. We admit it. We are not perfect; nor are our coworkers, family members, or spouse. The world does not work that way.

That's why we all need our Father. He is the answer—the only answer. He is our salvation. He is our only refuge. That is it. It is up to us to let go. We carry other people's problems, and it tires us. All we need to do is the best we can; let the rest go. Life is one big lesson, and this is ours. We cannot change others. We must save our own souls.

We get angry at ourselves for failing. Yes, we fail, but let's look at it differently. Have we not come very far? Have we not succeeded in many things? The answer is absolutely yes. So today, we see our failures and accept them as a stepping stone to our success—and yes, we are succeeding. Will we ever reach perfection? No, not upon this earth plane. Must we accept that? Yes. Can we be proud of our ever-increasing progress? Oh yes, and we are very happy with that. We accept our happiness, and now we move on. Then come failures, so we may learn and grow in our happiness.

WHAT IS CLEAR SIGHT?

We move just further into our lives, and see more evidence of an inept world, lost in its own thinking. It has no direction and no way out. It grumbles and spits back when spoken to for no reason. It shows its self-pity and wants us to feel sorry for it. It shows its stupidity, because it is immature. It shows its insincerity, because it is self-centered. It shows its insecurity, because it always wants to control. What a wasteful existence we have been upset with. Let us release our own insecurities and move on. Let us hold our head higher and be resolute. We are arriving at ourselves, and it feels good, sound, and right. We falter. We see our own fears, but as we do, we grow. In growing, we free ourselves from the bondage of wrong thinking.

Life is a grand stage of opportunity to learn that our Father truly loves us. He places all at our disposal to succeed. He just wants us to ask for help. Then, and only then, are we free and made whole. We are guided along the way through each step, each breath, each thought. Peace comes with the realization that we are not alone. We don't have to do it all by ourselves. All is well. We are loved and never abandoned. We surrender to our Father and are free.

WHAT IS SALVATION?

The journey deep within our soul offers us many surprises. We see the light shining through the darkness. It comforts us in our progress and urges us on. It is a matter of awareness that sets the stage for life. On the other hand, unclear vision produces anxiety, tenseness, and sorrow. Everyone struggles with this, and it can be seen in people's faces, the way they walk, and, of course, the way they act. The only truth is when we are true to ourselves. To be so takes a lot of gumption, and a tremendous amount of strength and faith. As we step through this thicket of forest's darkness, we sometimes cut ourselves. We are sometimes not sure of the way, but we keep going. As we keep going, we affirm ourselves and our heavenly Father. He has complete faith in us; why shouldn't we?

We all choose our paths of difficulty, but we are all armed with our own special gifts to overcome them. Our lives are meant to be very special, fulfilling, and outright joyous. Life offers us trials so we can overcome them and feel the sense of accomplishment that gives us confidence, joy, and peace. It is from this peace that we pass it on to others. With it, they are encouraged. Didn't anyone encourage us by their example? Didn't anyone take the time to listen to us? Didn't anyone take our hand and tell us everything would be all right? We are meant to have a joyous existence, not one filled with uncertainty and doubts and a sense of not feeling good enough. We need no longer entertain wrong thinking. Our Father gave us free will so we could decide to follow Him and realize the salvation of our souls. O' heavenly Father, hear us. Give us the strength to see the happiness You bestow upon us.

WHAT DOES TRUTH OFFER US?

We must train our mind not to entertain even mild anxiety. With new awareness, we transition to a new life with more fulfillment and joy. Awareness shows us the good and bad about ourselves and the world. With that clarity, we grow and relieve ourselves from burden. To not be "towed around" by life brings a relief, a peace that was once unimaginable. Truth carries a peace, but its value cannot be measured. Each step must be ours and no one else's. This is what brings us confidence, a lightness, and an appreciation of the flow of life. Nature changes; so must we. As we shed our rigidity, we become more at ease. Life starts to offer itself to us, and for that we are thankful.

WHAT IS THE MESSAGE?

The message is to be ourselves, enjoy the moment, and then move on without expectation. We let life show up. It always does so, anyway; we just deal with the good and the bad of it. We come upon this earth happy and content, and then spend the rest of our lives looking for happiness. What is wrong here? We got thrown out of the garden, and must earn our way back in. We let heaven fill our heart. The world is a tragedy. How we handle it is the *glory*. It takes faith, strength, and courage. In the process, we lose our innocence and must gain it back. It is only through the trials of life and our own free will that we turn back to our Father again and again. We consciously acknowledge Him and love Him. Through this choice and the granting of awareness, we are born again to Him. We follow our natural tendencies. We act in joy and abandonment. We are home.

HOW DO WE RECONCILE WITH THE WORLD?

As we wake up, we see the light. It shows us the world for more and more of what it is. The world is ugly and manipulative, and this stark reality has shaken us out of our stupor. We see more and more how unaware people are, and that fact causes an extreme amount of chaos and confusion in the world. This is what causes so much attack and "bad blood." We see more and more people simply wanted things their way. There is no give; if there is no give, there is no take. With that, no flow exists, so life stagnates. It is not creative. It is combative. When do we make our stand and be strong, and when do we give in? We are learning this, however slowly.

That's where our patience comes in. We must be patient. We must have strength. We must have faith. Without these, we will never be successful in our quest for freedom. May we hear Your voice, Father. May we heed Your help. When You tell us what to do, may we see the truth and know it. Life was not meant to be easy. It is meant to bring Your children back home to You, dear Father.

WHAT DECISION MUST WE MAKE TO LEAD A HAPPY AND FULFILLING LIFE?

Our thoughts and feelings rattle around inside us so strongly, at times, they give rise to a high level of anxiety. Why else would such feelings of tension arise, when there is no outward stimulation to trigger them? The weight of emotional stress we have carried for so many years is a nasty, insidious habit that holds on with all its force. It will not win, however, because our Father is with us, and only truth exists in us; so it is only truth we must focus on.

We look at our life and get disgruntled. We admit this. When we think and act this way, we are lacking faith. We are deciding to give our energy to our problems. This outlook has no value. It does not help us. It does not acknowledge who we really are. When we turn our attention to the truth about ourselves, we realize instead that we are intelligent, determined, courageous, and loved by our Father. No one has an easy time in life; that is not how life is designed. Life is designed so we can realize ourselves. Life is designed to make us strong. Life is designed to bring us back to our Father. The choice of being with our Father is the only answer. Everything else is a waste of time and energy. We are nothing without our Father, because we are Him. That is the truth. We are His children, who affirm His existence and posses His characteristics. It is our responsibility to save ourselves by realizing who we really are. We must decide. We cannot split ourselves between the world and Him. It must be a definite and absolute decision.

WHAT IS THE MOST IMPORTANT DECISION WE NEED TO MAKE?

Why do we eternally stay in conflict? Are our ignorance and unwillingness the reasons for such sorrow, which comes as we continually tear at ourselves for the answers? We need to make choices for our own happiness; only we can do this. We cry out at our creation of being a victim and look at the cruelty of the world as the intruder to our peace. Are these thoughts correct? Are we not in command of our life, by making the right choices for ourselves? Are not our thoughts dictators of our reality? Did indeed our Father give us the capacity to chart our destiny and the strength to live it? So why do we wait in conflict and endure the suffering?

It is fear that keeps us in toe, and leads us around in circles of doubt. Instead, our mandate is to rise above the din of noisy thoughts of confusion and be blessed by our innate character and true Spirit. To recognize the Spirit of our Father within ourselves releases us from the fear we carry in our own mind. It is only through our choice of surrender to our Father that we move beyond the conflict of trying to decide to do the right thing. Are we not the right thing? Are we not heavenly? Are we not truly the reflection of our Father's light? The holiness of our Father is imparted by Him with impartiality. We all are Him. We all reflect His qualities. We choose instead to wander and squander our abilities, trying to be safe and comfortable. This is where the conflict gives rise. We search for safety where there is none. We run after pleasure to avoid pain that we feel from the separation to our Father.

We must choose to be with our Father. We must choose now, for now is the eternity we live in. Our Father waits for us, and we have refused Him. We have distracted ourselves with wishful thinking and self-pity. No one else can make it all right. Instead, the matter lies in not putting our faith in the chaos. No one knows what they are doing, unless they have committed to our Father. The conflict causes great sorrow, and, if harbored, resentment. We must look deep into our own heart and soul, and make our decision to move from thoughts of conflict and attack to thoughts of harmony and good fortune. Only our Father can grant us this peace. If we entertain any thoughts of yearning, we will wander and never find fulfillment. Instead, the choice is clear. Faith in our Father is our only sane option. Will the road be smooth and easy? No, but the road will be sure, with no doubts caused by conflict. By surrendering to our Father, we will know—absolutely know—who we are, and wander no more.

HOW DO WE SEE THE TRUTH ABOUT OURSELVES?

With every step we take, we feel triumph and see more of the truth. The more aware we become, the more we see the patterns of our behavior; by doing that, we see the ugliness of the pain we cause ourselves. We also see more of other people's unconsciousness. The more we see, the uglier it looks. But, in the ugliness, is there not hope? Cannot the chains of sadness be broken? Cannot we climb out of this web of entanglement that has trapped us our entire lives? This is an opportunity for victory and a freedom from misconceptions, which we replace with freethinking and a genuine respect for ourselves and others. We must face the ugly truth. We must face it head-on. It is only with our Father's grace that we can drop these ugly, disdainful thoughts from our minds and walk free to live our lives the way we want, at the same time hurting no one.

HOW DO WE FREE OURSELVES FROM THE PAST?

There is a sorrow that comes over us at times, and we do not know where it comes from. However, if we really listen to ourselves, we do know. Impressionable, negative moments from our childhood haunt our thoughts and color our lives. We still keep our feelings buried. They do come up—slowly, but they do come up. When they do, we must admit to them, and finally let them go. Our lives literally depend on it. We must admit what happened to ourselves as small children and accept it. It is only when we accept it that we can forgive ourselves and those we feel perpetrated against us. This transformation must occur, for us to have peace. We ask now our holy Father for help, to accept our cross and cleanse our soul. We ask to see with clarity our own errors. We ask for help to forgive ourselves for not feeling worthy enough, smart enough, or capable enough. It is time now to move on to happiness and leave the sorrow behind. We must be proud of ourselves and who we are. It is time for us to take command of our lives. We must start somewhere. The first step is to accept; the second is to forgive. The sorrow must go; it does not belong with us anymore. It has no place with us.

HOW DO WE HANDLE CONFRONTATION?

Just by the way it sounds, confrontation seems like a bad word. It does not have to be that way, though, does it? Confrontation can be done in a positive way. So, what does that *mean*—in a positive way?

It means when we speak our mind, we just speak our mind. We do not threaten the other person. Instead, we bring light to the subject at hand. If we confront someone with our honest feelings, they have the choice to respond to us in kind. If we never tell them how we feel, they will never know.

Now, some people will lie and try to manipulate us. People that want us as a customer will be nice to us, because they want our money. Others will just be nice to us. The best approach is to tell someone, with honesty, how we feel. If we are true to ourselves, we are in a much better position to know how the other person feels. If they respond in kind—with respect and from their own sense of dignity—we have an even exchange of ideas, which leads to a mutual agreement and a benefit for both people involved.

If the other person continues to talk to manipulate us, we have a choice. We can let them do so, or we can confront them again. If they become angry with us, it is a good sign they are trying to do us wrong. If they talk forever, it is a sign they are trying to manipulate us. If they cry and say "poor me," they are manipulating us as well. If they become really upset in a rage, they want us to fold. Awareness is our friend here. We must be as true to ourselves as our awareness allows us. Then, we are way ahead of the game of life.

It appears that the lies and manipulation have the upper hand and all the rewards of life; however, that is not so. Liars toil and work at their own deceptions, in order to uphold themselves. The truth always prevails; in reality, that is all there is. The truth is eternal and forever. The deception withers away; it has no substance. It is made up. It is not of our Father. It has no real power. We must first confront ourselves before we can confront others. We must be honest in who we are and what we see in ourselves. We must confront the thoughts in our mind that haunt us and trouble our soul. We must confront the sadness that strangles our heart. We must confront the anxiety that colors our world. We must confront the fear that keeps us from our happiness. We face it head-on, with dignity and respect for ourselves. It is only in that way that we can also confront our brothers and sisters.

Our Father reigns here. Does our Father confront? No; He does not need to confront anything, because everything that is real is Him. Why should He confront Himself? It makes no sense. So, until we are one with Him, we must confront our own devils until we believe in them no more. Then, instead of confronting our brothers and sisters, we will see them as part of ourselves, so conflict and confrontation will not exist. An exchange will occur; in that exchange, awareness will grow between ourselves and others. Godlike qualities and our Father's blessings will grow, and so will we.

HOW IS THE TRUTH ABOUT OURSELVES SUSTAINED?

There is a fascination with people-watching that never grows old. It must be the uniqueness with which our Father created all of us. We truly reflect—or is it project—all our thoughts and feelings onto the rest of the world. As others' projections meet with ours, a like or dislike occurs; in other words, a judgment. From that point, we make decisions on what to say or do. That has a false basis, however, because judgment should not come into the picture. The truth has no judgment. So how does one not judge? We are true to ourselves. We honor our uniqueness, no matter what others' projections or judgments are placed on us. In that way, we express naturally, and that is what others do not like; they cannot see their own nature. They take it as an affront, an attack, and they try to destroy our truth. This cannot be done. When we are true to ourselves, we can never be destroyed. This we must believe.

WHEREIN LIES THE TRUTH?

At times, we feel dismayed, but this we cause ourselves. Our Father does not desire this for us. This occurs when we refuse Him. This occurs when we have lack of faith. This occurs when we do not want to accept who we really are. There is an abundance in our lives right now that we are not accepting. Why are we doing that? We must drop this belief; then, all will be aright. All these doubts and emotions come from not truly believing in our Father. His masterful way for us is all-encompassing. We cannot escape it, although we fool ourselves and think we can. This causes sorrow, when we wish for things that will never happen. It is the undoing of these beliefs that reveals our freedom. This world is a vehicle by which we must learn to choose the truth. We must ask for our Father's strength to face the truth. In the light of the truth, we are free, unhampered, and filled with a rich happiness and peace. Life turns from sorrow to joy. Heaven is a true realization. The choice is ours to make. It is a personal decision no one else can make for us. This is what is meant by free will. We let heaven come. If it must come step by step, we are grateful. With each step, the veil is lifted, and we see more and more the truth of who we really are. Life is ours. We are life. Our Father granted us life. We must accept it. We must be happy with what we have and who we are. There lies the truth. We are the truth, and we now accept it.

HOW DO WE REALIZE WE ARE TRULY OUR FATHER'S CHILDREN?

It cannot be forced; peace just comes naturally, and it comes directly from our Father. As we express ourselves to others, it gives us a better sense of where people stand. As we are more true to ourselves, we see others with more and more clarity. Some are lost, some are sorrowful, some are nice, and some are outright self-centered and manipulative. There cannot be a separation from our brothers and sisters; that would be impossible. They are like us, children of our Father. We are one. The point here is realizing we are all our Father's children. That is the quest of all of us, who suffer in pain because we do not see Him and do not truly see ourselves.

Life's lessons teach us who we are. If we do not want to accept who we are, the tragedy of attack and manipulation remain a constant battle in our hearts and minds. This remains, until we surrender to our true nature by giving up the madness. Only shame exists, if we do not believe in ourselves—if we do not *know* ourselves. We feel guilty when we do something wrong. Well, what is wrong? Who says something is wrong? Who has that authority over us? Are we not our own masters? Are we not the very essence of our Father? If we are true to our own nature, we are never wrong. We are ourselves, who are truly our Father's co-creators, who are continually learning and expanding ourselves. False beliefs set us up to be captives of ourselves. Dropping them, we live in harmony with ourselves and in the real world of happiness. This means we have the opportunity to create and express ourselves, unhampered and free— with no inhibitions, guilt, shame, or doubt. The blessings of our Father are ours. We just need to realize and accept them. Life is wonderful in this true existence; it offers us a grand sharing with our heavenly Father.

WHAT DOES OUR FATHER NEED FROM US?

As the awareness comes, the fear slips away. In its stead lie confidence and peace. It is a naturalness—so soothing, it gives pause to why we struggle at all. Any trial or hardship that befalls us is literally a wake-up call to awareness. It is rising from a warm bed and stepping into a cold shower. The stunning and overwhelming events of our life are meant to awaken us to ourselves. With just a hint of willingness to overcome these obstacles, we put into motion the path to our freedom. We are never alone; how can we be? We are of our Father and always will be.

As the veil of outright illusion drops from our mind, we see a brighter day filled with us being who we truly are. We must know in our darkest hour that the Light is just a whisper away. It is faith that brings us there. It is faith in our Father and faith in ourselves. This is the Kingdom. The beauty of the matter is we don't have to do anything but be willing, and believe, *really* believe. Then we need to listen, *really* listen, to our own hearts. Then, we must follow our own promptings. The rest, our Father takes care of. The way is made clear; all we have to do is walk it, with dignity and faith in our Almighty Father. His riches are truly abundant, and *very* powerful. He helps those who believe in Him. He must be first and foremost in our heart and mind. He comes above spouse, children, family, and friends. Then and only then are we saved.

Our salvation is in our own hands, and only true belief in our heavenly Father will grant it to us. Everything else we hold is false beliefs we think will make us happy. We light up our life today—right now. We stretch out our hand to our Father. He is waiting in eternity for us. He needs us to see Him. We make Him happy and He rejoices. We feel the wholeness inside ourselves of truly being one with our heavenly Father, right with ourselves, and right with the world.

WHAT IS BEHIND THE VEIL?

Sometimes, our thoughts come with so much clarity, the puzzle of life we see day in and day out resolves itself. We vacillate between feelings of impossibility and feelings of calm and assuredness. As we pray, we calm ourselves. We can see and feel the strength of our Father within us. The relief is beyond words. We feel settled and capable; no problem or task seems so large and daunting anymore. We ask ourselves today about our own dignity, because this is what we have been seeking all of our life. We see our lack of self-respect and our reaction to other people's wishes, as if our whole world will end unless we please them, bend to their will, and keep them happy. But alas! They will never be happy, and neither will we if we continue this charade, run by their egos and our own.

This way of living causes confusion, regrets, anger, and resentment. Now, we must pray for strength and guidance. Our perceptions are tainted with false beliefs for happiness. We feel this veil of deception and tears crumbling, yet our impatience sets expectations for instant results. What a pity and what a mistake! It's useless to feel this way. The ego is tenacious, with all its attempts to keep itself intact. Yet it has no power over our Father. The choice is always clear, and yet we stay in this misery and vacillate with our intentions. However, we now pray to our Father to give us strength, to see His face, to touch His hand, and walk with Him as we fill ourselves with His life. As we entertain these words, it brings us peace. Just the thought of Him settles us. This is what we must do. We pray to Him and never give up faith in Him. He lays obstacles before us to make us stronger. He tries our patience so we may grow in love. Then he sees His beautiful child. In this way, we honor Him.

HOW DO WE SEE OUR TRUE SELF?

We feel a sense of relief today. The peace comes after we face our problems and fears. Yes, this is being true to ourselves. As we choose our true nature and feelings, peace comes. We must risk all we hold dear to know our Father. The illusions of the world, we have held very dear to ourselves. This falseness causes the pain. So, as we let these false notions and beliefs go, we find the peace we are looking for. We can put no earthly value on contentment and peace. It lightens our load from the heavy thoughts we allow to weigh on our mind and heart.

We cannot control the world, but we can control ourselves. We can control our own thoughts and feelings. In this way, we make a choice. We exercise our free will to choose to accept our Father. We choose to see ourselves for who we really are. Heaven *does* rest in the midst of ourselves. It is only through the strength of our Father that we can realize our true heritage. We humble ourselves before Him. We simply ask, and He happily grants us the strength to see Him, see Him with clarity. He waits for us. All we need to do is ask for His help.

HOW IS OUR LIFE'S CONDITIONING CHANGED?

The turmoil is more abrupt and apparent. We see it more consistently. We watch ourselves foster it and encourage its growth. It lays in germination, waiting for the slightest ripple in life to set it off. Our awareness of it becomes more and more prominent. We allow other people and circumstances to set us off in anger, frustration, worry, and aggravation. We give our power away when we do this. We are not seeing our True Self. If we did, we would not be in turmoil. We ask our Father to help us drop our past life and instead see our strength, so we can let go of these false beliefs. We ask our Father for the strength and love to express ourselves. In this way, we will no longer carry the burden that ravages our mind, emotions, and heart. We ask our Father to help us hear Him clearly, see his light, and live in the peace that is His gift to us.

WHAT DOES IT MEAN TO BE ALIGNED TO OUR FATHER?

The vast universe we see before us emanates from ourselves. Its ebb and flow is our ebb and flow. As we align ourselves to it, we no longer fight it. The results of our thoughts and actions become more creative and productive, and the weight of misery and suffering recedes from our mind and heart. The road seems long; yet, in reality, no step is needed. We simply wake up to life, as it rewards us with its blessings. The holiness of our Father is exposed to us, and the truth brings into focus the everlasting goodness of our Father, as His free-flowing love is bestowed upon His children. Our heart lightens as we realize this. The cruelties of the world pale in the light of our Father's goodness. We are Him, and in that realization, we claim the Almighty within ourselves and rest in the peace of His infinite love.

WHAT IS TRUE COMMITMENT TO OUR FATHER?

There can be no doubt in our mind about our Father and His eternal and infinite love for us. If we have one inkling of doubt, we don't have Him. He is completely committed to us, and we must be completely committed to Him. This is true love. This is unconditional love. This is faith in the unseen power of the universe. This is how mountains are moved. The world has no power. It only moves to the whims of gigantic egos that drive the rest of the lambs to the slaughter. The righteousness of our Father always exists. Complete faith in our Father and His love for us allows us to see that. We surrender to who we really are with complete faith. Only in that way will be live completely.

WHY IS LIFE SO DIFFICULT?

We were meant to take this, our path. We picked it for ourselves. It is a strength builder, and it stretches our soul to the point of making us more aware of our shortcomings, which we now address. We question ourselves incessantly, and then also take a look at how well we are doing. It is a very silly exercise. It holds no value. We expect perfection the first time out. Isn't that ridiculous? It is like wanting to be a crack pilot the first time we get in the cockpit. Life just doesn't work that way.

Life presents itself to us, and by surrendering ourselves to our Father, we find the answers to deal with life. We then make our way on our own terms. It is a continual process with no end, and there should not be an end. Why? Because life is everlasting. It is creation itself. It is our Father's love, which He shares with us. We must teach ourselves to share in His goodness and in His life. So we say: "come, life's lessons." Teach us to see life for what it is. Help us to heal our mind and heart. Let us create, unhampered by inhibitions and fears. We are our Father's children. His power is our power. All of His good is our good. The more we express and share His good, the more we realize who we are. So then, we say to life's lessons: "knock the chafe from our mind and heart. Set us free."

WHAT MUST WE DO TO SUCCEED?

It is a test of faith and commitment to our Father and ourselves. He calls us to do our best, for our best reflects Him. He sees us for who we truly are. He provides us the gift of determination, courage, and humor to light our way back to Him. As the light becomes brighter, our way is made more clear. Our journey reflects less struggle and more achievement. We must keep our mind with positive thoughts as we hit up against obstacles and things people do that we do not like. This gives us the opportunity to create a clear path. In prayer, we can do this. This is the ultimate assurance. Our Father never fails, so He will never fail us. Belief in this provides true security and assured success.

HOW ARE WE RESPONSIBLE FOR OUR OWN REALITY?

As we become more clear about the reality of our own world, it brings more of an acute focus to our strengths and weaknesses. So, as we recognize our strengths and finally admit to our God-given talents, we must also admit to the weaknesses that create the problems in our lives. It is not a rosy picture in this earthly world, at least in our lifetime. The good and bad we were given, as well as what we cultivated during our lives, set our reality. With more clarity, we make right decisions; with less clarity, we flounder and become more confused. We must always remember to pray, even though the pace of our lives accelerates.

Only through communion with our Father does clarity come. With faith and focus, anything is available to us. This is how our thoughts move through the universe and shape it into our happiness. There is no need to worry. Our Father is always present and all-powerful. So in this, our contrition, we beg for our Father's mercy and love to touch us and wake us up to Him. His strength is our security. His love is our only comfort. His sight is our only clarity. Only in this way may we see the truth about ourselves and the world we create to live in.

WHAT DOES IT MEAN TO BE IN THE MOMENT?

When the instant is gone, the instant is gone. It cannot be recaptured with the same feelings and intensity. It cannot be sought after for what it once was. It no longer exists. Therefore, happiness is found right now. It surely cannot be found in the past, although memories can soothe our soul as well as haunt us. We cannot find happiness in the future, because we truly do not know what the future is. That, no one really knows. So here we are in the present moment, with our own thoughts and feelings. From this point, we embark on life's journey over and over again. This is the opportunity to live freely and in harmony. The present is unencumbered by past transgressions or happiness of a time gone by; this cannot be recaptured, nor is it meant to be. Life is truly eternal, since it always exists. It exists in this very moment—and there always is a moment, isn't there? We are not defunct one moment and alive the next. We simply exist. So the next time someone asks "how are you?" we need not grind our teeth about the past, whether due to years gone by or stubbing our toe this morning. We meet others in the very moment and reflect our true feelings to them right there. We reach for the happiness that is truly in our soul right now.

HOW DO WE ASK FOR OUR FATHER'S HELP?

Our lives stand before us with more clarity; this is what we have asked of our Father. He delivers unconditionally what we ask of Him, only if it is good for us. If we do not ask with truth and honesty, He cannot grant what we ask. He calls on us to respond with truth. In honesty and truth to ourselves, we realize the answers we need to live a better and more fulfilling life. As the clarity comes, we see a more vibrant world. We also see more people's faces filled with pain and loneliness. We see the physical attractions of the world that bears their temptations. We see the fabric of our past life and the shaping of our character and why we are the way we are.

Our Father grants us our desire to know more of the mysteries of life. We also ask Him to give us strength to see them. Holy, holy is His name. Our faith must be strengthened, for us to endure. Our confidence must be built, for us to achieve. Our love must grow, for us to understand. Our strength must rise, for us to avoid temptations. Our humility must deepen, for us to ask for our Father's help. We pray now for these gifts that sustain us.

HOW ARE BURDENS LIFTED?

The burdens we all carry seem immense. We let our problems weigh us down, tire us, and put us in turmoil. This is an egocentric viewpoint; it holds us in the ego's grasp and points us toward the ultimate burden of the fear of death and death itself. Faith, however, is the antidote of this burden we carry in our hearts and minds. Faith lifts us out of this warped thinking into the light of hope, positivity, and a complete devotion to our Father. Only when we see who we are, truly are, is the burden lifted. Only through complete humility do we find our way. We do not beg. We do not plead. We ask in humility and complete surrender.

We take heed of our Father's answer, and then take action. Only in this way will we lift this burden. We let each moment present itself, and, armed with our faith, we naturally know what to do. Only by looking deeply inside ourselves for the truth and asking our Father for help will the burdens be lifted. Also, as we proceed moment by moment, we are relieved from temptations. No room exists for them to come in. Temptations are evoked from egocentric thinking. Egocentric thinking is anchored in the past. We must be courageous. We take the proverbial leap of faith. We trust ourselves to carry out the answers that are Father provides us when we ask. Righteousness is a gift. Truth is the answer, and life is for us to enjoy without measure and burden.

WHAT IS OUR TRUE REALITY?

The vast expanse of the universe is a sign to us of our own vast talents and capabilities. The natural order of the universe also is inherent in us. The beauty of the universe is also the beauty that shines in our very soul. The acceptance of ourselves and the knowledge of who we truly are is the greatest gift we can grant ourselves. Our Father's helping hand guides us to ultimate fulfillment, where all is right and life flows along with the universe and its natural order. Anything else that comes into the picture of our mind is false in its intention and clutters our mind with minuscule wants and needs that are not really ours.

As we dispel these nagging wants and needs, we feel the weight rescinding. We move as a free agent in the world, which affords us unending possibilities. Life is truly meant to be enjoyed in all circumstances, both difficult and easy. Holy is our Father that permeates all creation, including ourselves, and waits in patient existence with love and care for us. We turn our back to this all-encompassing existence when we turn our thoughts away from Him to our own small thoughts and desires for comfort or an easier way. Our universe is there for us inside our mind and heart, ready to be explored in its entirety. Only by choosing our innate heritage of freedom will we awaken to the manifestation of our Father's good in us, which waits to rise up and express itself. Through creation, we live and breathe Him. In truth, we are Him.

HOW IS FEAR FACED?

As we look into the din of fear, we see its useless turmoil and tormenting ways. Its grip strengthens as we let it, and it takes over and paralyzes us from right action, correct decisions, and the truth that we deny ourselves in our heart. Only through the strength of our Father does fear dissipate and finally disappear. The comfort of not facing fear only increases its power and hold over us. It can be devastating, if we let it.

The facts must be faced, for our freedom to be gained. Only through our Father's strength will we overcome the fear that grips us and causes us such extreme turmoil and unhappiness. Fear does not provide us a "cozy comfort." Instead, it covers our mind from seeing our Father. It creates a huge illusion to keep us in its grip. It is only through the strength of our Father that we can rise above this illusion. Our Father's love must totally reign in our heart, without question and any hint of doubt. Faith is a driving force. Faith is acquired by devoted prayer. Only through honesty in ourselves can we see our heavenly Father. We must be true to ourselves, not only in what we want to do, but also in what we see within ourselves, both good and bad. Fear must be overcome for the victory of freedom to be won. Freedom is won, not through self-righteousness or arrogance, but instead through accepting ourselves as we are, with all our strengths, talents, and abilities, as well as our weaknesses and shortcomings.

The path we take is no longer giving in to people's insecurities, instead voicing our view with honesty, directness, and respect for ourselves and them. We cannot let them push us around. When we commit to our Father, that will cease to happen. Little by little, as our faith grows, we will lose our insecurities. By facing up to people with their insecurities, we will change our world and theirs, so the light of our Father will shine more brightly in it. True life is life in the light and love of our Almighty Father.

WHAT IS ACCEPTANCE?

Acceptance only comes through our own willingness. People don't change for us, and we should not expect them to. People change for themselves. As we each decide to make our own way back home to our Father, we realize the true identity in each other. We are all precious, intelligent, and limitless human beings. The tragedy of not being aware of this fact causes ourselves and others huge problems at home, work, and, most flagrantly, in the world at large.

Acceptance brings peace. In being more at peace, we naturally offer it to others. This allows them to relax their guard and give us what we want. What we want is more peace. As barriers recede between intelligent souls, creativity flows more freely. Problems become resolved more quickly and easily. Life flows from one to another, and happiness emerges. Our natural state emerges, as we listen to our hearts. As we listen to our hearts, we accept life for what it is. As we accept life for what it is, we move more freely. Everyone succeeds. To the extent we are true to ourselves, life offers its blessings to us. So our mandate is to look deep within our hearts, and accept both our great talents and human weaknesses. We then accept them equally, with the same amount of love and understanding. We need to neither pump ourselves up with our accomplishments, nor downgrade ourselves with our failures. We need simply to accept who we are, and move to our own promptings. Then, life will be truly acceptable.

WHAT IS THE NATURE OF LIFE?

Thoughts come to us to keep pushing, keep looking, and keep struggling. Yet, we know this is erroneous thinking. It is thinking that hangs on insecurities and fears. It is a projection from our past, and it colors and haunts our future. As we come to new realizations, it evokes a freedom, a freedom of choice. Free choice in the present connects us to a brighter future—whatever that future may turn out to be.

Life is a continuum of moments laid out before us as a gift to be explored, which offers us our full potential. Full potential only exists in the moment, because it carries no weight or preconception from the past. Anything is possible in the moment. Anything can happen. Anything can be realized. Anything can be ours to explore. We, being in the moment, are therefore connected to life itself. As it flows, we flow. If we are flowing, we are creating; thus, we are living. If we are living, we are truly in heaven on earth. Our godlike qualities are expressed, and by our expression, we are sharing them. By sharing, we are expanding our Father's love. So then, as we give, we truly receive; life expands for us, and the nature of life is expansion. By adhering to the natural law of life to expand, we become more and more at peace. We are an eternal, limitless, expanding being, living as a human upon this earth. Happiness comes from this peace. We are not only part of life, we are life itself.

WHAT MUST WE DO TO BE COMPLETELY FREE?

Being upset comes from inward turmoil. No one and nothing can upset us if we do not carry thoughts and feelings of inner conflict, fear, and uncertainty. As we become more aware and allow ourselves the right to be in the moment, our false perceptions drop, and we are free to think and act in a positive, creative, and productive way. We are truly limitless in what we can do and experience. In the same light, we are also invulnerable, because by allowing our innocence to meet the moment, we cause no threat to anyone or our surroundings. By just being, we walk freely.

The alternative is dim, and offers us confusion, fear, and the entrapment of hell itself. So we ask ourselves, literally, "what on earth do we do?" The fact of the matter and the answer, of course, lie deep within us. The gift of free will offers us the choice to claim our salvation. No compromise must exist here. Our decision must be flat out and absolutely seated in our mind and heart. We need to make the decision to do it whether it is falling to our knees, bowing reverently, or prostrating ourselves on the ground. We must absolutely commit ourselves to our Father with all the faith we can muster, and

He will grant us the riches we so ache to possess. When we believe this with our whole heart, the world will lay at our feet.

HOW DO WE KNOW WHAT TO DO WITH OUR LIVES?

We watch ourselves pushing to no avail, and it causes us more strain, which causes us turmoil. The ideas that come to us, we must evaluate for validity. If we pursue them, we must really want to; it must be worth our effort. We must ask ourselves if we are doing it out of fear, to get assurances, or to be well informed, so we can make intelligent decisions. Our energy is precious, because it comes from our Father. We do not need to squander it needlessly on pursuits we believe will temper our fears. Life is meant to be enjoyed in a positive light. The energy we exert must be for a pursuit we are genuinely interested in partaking in. Running around, trying to make everything safe and perfect, is a waste of energy and fruitless. Our mandate to ourselves is to trust life. We can only do that by trusting ourselves. Releasing the past allows us to cheer up, and we see our life filled with positivity and possibilities. We still can observe and honor our usual approach to our pursuits, but we can drop the fears and uncertainties.

Life offers us opportunities upon opportunities to release ourselves of pain, and create a world for ourselves that nourishes us and therefore nourishes others. In this way, we are true to ourselves. Happiness is ours, as we seize each moment to move forward instead of moving back to the past, hauling it with us as we make our way through life. If our ideas are sound and true, we will naturally pursue them. If they are based in fear and a search for assurances, they must be released; they have no meaning. Life is meant to be lived in the fullness of each moment, with dignity and courage. We must let our intuition be our guide and then pursue what we really want. Those who really love us will encourage us to do that. Our life must be lived fully, and we can only do that by being true to our own ideas and evaluating our intent.

WHY MUST WE ASK OUR FATHER FOR HELP?

It is a matter of faith. We allow our mind to be preoccupied with wasteful and unnecessary thoughts. They drain our energy and rob us of the enjoyment we seek. We are not present if our mind is wandering in a maze of wants in the future or thoughts of personal affronts against us in the past. Life possesses a joy that cannot be lived unless the madness of the mind ceases. Faith is the antidote to madness, and prayer builds that faith—prayer that rises from humility and truly asks our Father for help. Only from this can peace come. Only then, can the creative ideas fill our mind. We even need to ask our Father for the courage to act on these ideas. We need to ask our Father for everything. That likely grates on us, but that is how life works. Our Father *is* life. He is our source. Do we need to go to Him to be nourished? Is He not wanting to hear our call for help? Does He not want us back home with Him? He never refuses us; if He did, He would be refusing Himself, and that is impossible.

So, in the same spirit we ask, we must receive. We act on His answers in complete faith. We act on them in the moment. We don't ask for our future bread or our past bread. We ask for our "daily bread." The enjoyment of life comes daily, not from tomorrow's wishes and not from memories of yesterday. Faith is the answer. We must trust our Father and love Him completely with no reservations, and our daily existence will be filled with strength, enlightenment, and the joy of the continual and ever-renewing realization of ourselves.

HOW IS OUR SADNESS RELIEVED?

We are seeing ourselves for more and more of who we really are. We created our life so far, and we are creating our life right now. As we change our mind, our life changes. As we worry, it colors our life with fear of the future. As we relieve ourselves from the way things are and how we see them continuing poorly, it can only soothe our soul.

Acceptance and courage are our powerful allies. We cannot change others, but we can change ourselves. As we accept others and circumstances, we relieve ourselves from the weight of not having things the way we want them. Is this the path to happiness? Have we really been ignoring this fact, and not wanting to face it? Is this why we see sadness in our own lives? Beauty and peace lie within us. It is up to us to have the courage to see them and allow ourselves the right to happiness. What is a good life? How do we define that for ourselves? It is faith that gives us relief.

The answer is to stop searching, but instead awaken. The answer is not to push, but instead to appreciate. The answer is not to stay in sorrow and say "if only," but instead to decide we really want to be happy with ourselves and our life right now. That is thanksgiving, and that is abundance. We ask our Father, although we have little faith for Him to hear our call. We ask Him to relieve us from the doubts and outward appearances of our life and give us the courage to allow Him to nurture us with His love. Only by accepting our Father's love will we get relief.

HOW DO WE CHOOSE LOVE OVER FEAR?

The madness we see in the world is unending. No solace lives in it at all. A perpetual wall of fear fragments it, one human being from another. Out of this fear, frustration and anger protrude their ugly heads and roar with a deafening volume. Then, through that noise, no one can be heard. Only through a sense of peace in ourselves can cooperation and life with others be lived. No other way exists. Fear builds on fear, into a whirlwind of destruction. Fear also evokes doubt, anxiety, and depression, which is a form of self-destruction. This fear is thrust inward, causing self-destruction, and eventually outward to the destruction of the world.

So then, where does happiness come into the picture? In this huge den of iniquity, does happiness have a chance? Can happiness coexist with an insane and vicious world? Well, of course not. So it is our realization to choose a life of peace, contentment, and happiness in the light of our Father. Only through faith and *great strength* can we walk on this earth and "be in it, but not of it," We must and do exist in our Father's world. That is the real world; the other does not really exist. It is a fantasy in the minds of many who delude themselves and walk around asleep as lost souls. It is only through faith that we truly live. It is only through faith that we realize our true nature. It is only through faith that we know our Father. All else is nonsense, and it will destroy itself in the end.

HOW DOES HEALING OCCUR?

The truth hurts, as we come to the realization of it. It burns with clarity, and sets into motion a healing process. The pain is excruciating, because the crookedness of our thoughts no longer has a place to hide. They stand exposed, naked and no longer covered by the comfortable blanket of deception. From this viewpoint, spiritual pain is more extreme than physical pain; the only way to heal it is to dive right into it, like a crusader. We must be valiant, upright, and kind with our approach. Gaining heaven relies upon the right approach of strength, understanding, and compassion.

Long-standing issues of dependency and weakness hurt the most. The deformity and entanglement have grown comfortable over the years, and their undoing causes strained pain. Sometimes, it possesses an unending dullness; sometimes, it rises up with a sharpness that can cause further irritation and sorrow. We stand, vulnerable and open, but now instead we are armed with awareness and our Father's sustaining help. We let no tear be shed in self-pity, but instead in healing. We let no word come from anger, but instead from truth and thanksgiving. We let no thought rise and take over what will deepen a wound or worsen an injury. Instead, we continually ask for guidance and strength. We ask for authority, laced with the strength of compassion and understanding. We must be at peace in our thoughts. We keep our Father ever present in our mind. We walk with confidence, as our Father's child. We must forever stay on our quest of doing our Father's will. This is the only way the pain will heal itself and disintegrate into nothingness. What is left? That is what was always there. It is the truth of our Father's love for each and every one of us.

HOW DO WE RELEASE THE PAST?

We burden ourselves unnecessarily with thoughts of worry, frustration, and aggravation. We hang onto them with a sense of searching for answers we believe lie within them. We look in the past for answers to the present, and in that exercise, we falter and frustrate ourselves once again. It is in the endless cycle of wanting, which *only* perpetuates our own sorrow. In this sorrow, we once found our refuge. It provided us a comfort of familiarity, as we lay down in its cozy bed. Why do we even entertain these thoughts now? Why do we linger in the servitude of misery and confusion? Our life has turned to brighter days, just as the sun raises its head in the mornings to light the day's activities. We feel a "jumble" in our soul and inner thoughts. Is this a sign of release? There is a "jangling" of incoherence. Are we letting something go? Has our journey led us to another point of resolution?

We want and want and want, to no avail. We yearn, and come up empty-handed. We look to the past for answers, and find no reprieve. We ask our Father, what must we do? How do we know our own truth? Where do we go to find answers? Where will our life's journey take us? There are many questions, and really no good answers. Life demands courage. Courage demands faith. Faith demands trust. Trust demands commitment. Commitment demands love. Love does not demand, but simply gives. We must learn this. We must relinquish preconceived notions and then, with our heavenly Father, walk with the trust of a child, the courage of a mighty warrior, and a focused commitment as if our life depended on it; it truly does. O' holy Father, help us to relinquish our past today.

HOW DOES WORRY END?

Our prayers do not go unanswered. As we realize more, we come to a better understanding, and that settles us down. It gives us hope, and encourages us to continue on our infinite journey. As we understand more, events and people affect us less. We are more aware of others' wandering minds, as our mind becomes more settled. We still allow ourselves to be concerned about loved ones, although worry is not a benefit to them or ourselves. For this, we need to pray for more strength. For it is our Father's will that we will need all our strength when the time comes to care for them. Our blessings abide in our consciousness as we start to see the landscape of the world and our life itself. We have searched for nourishment in the fantasies of our own mind. We have waited impatiently and searched incessantly, with an intolerable yearning for happiness. Yet, in this way, we push our happiness away. It lies instead taunting us, just outside our reach.

We find that our salvation only lies in our Father. He tells us to relax, enjoy, and stop the stress we lay upon ourselves. Victory only lies in Him. Through an evolution of ourselves, we see our own shortcomings and observe an uncomfortable stressfulness, even on an uneventful day. Does this not measure what we are doing to ourselves? Are we not instead acknowledging our monumental accomplishments and blessings? In these, we can find the nourishment we seek. Do we not have health? Do we not have family? Do we not have financial resources and means? Do we go hungry or look to where we might spend the night? Do we not have dear ones that love us? We must wake up and enjoy our life. We must laugh every day and smile at the good and the bad. In reality, we live eternally with our Father. We ask Him to strengthen our faith so we might see Him more clearly, every day and in each moment. We must relax and enjoy life.

WHAT IS TRUST?

What does trusting life really mean? Where does that trust come from? How is trust achieved? Who bestows this trust? When is this trust realized? Why does this trust matter? The essence here is understanding our true nature and our divine relationship to our Father. The spark of life we feel deep within our soul is the light that illumines the way. Heaven awaits us in eternity, with arms open and outstretched. Our Father calls us constantly to pick ourselves up out of the mire and drudgery of everyday existence into the fulfillment of the promise of who we really are.

Now, how can this be accomplished? What must we do to take our rightful place in the Kingdom of our Father? This small but mighty step comes from the release of fear. As fear is dropped, light dawns on our mind and rests in our heart. The easiness of life presents itself in a soft wonderment, as we awaken from our slumber of dullness, apathy, and the clenches of fear itself.

As we trust ourselves, we trust life. How can this trust be gained? It is only through prayer and complete commitment to our Father that life will be open to us. We walk with humility and dignity. We choose the light in every moment. We stop wandering. We stop wallowing in fear and self-doubt. We step out into life and meet it fully, head-on, and with a cheerful spirit. Heaven is our choice, and the trust we put in our Father and ourselves is the answer to our continual fulfillment of the reality of truth. We must be true to ourselves in all circumstances. We must love ourselves through all defeats as well as triumphs. We must keep our head up, no matter what faces us, and laugh at ourselves to lighten our load. We must choose positive and enriching thoughts and throw out any ideas that squelch the fire of the true love within us. In this way, we take on life for what it truly is. For this, we are forever thankful to our Almighty and loving Father, who is life itself.

HOW IS ACCEPTANCE ACHIEVED?

We talk to our Father, and then listen to His response. When we ask in honesty, He responds to us. He told us to accept others just the way they are, to accept circumstances just the way they are, and finally to accept ourselves just the way we are. That is called love, true love, for it is unconditional. It is also accepting the facts of life. So the pining to have things another way only causes turmoil; it covers up, and therefore negates happiness. Life is meant to be engaged, no matter what. From our Father's hand, we were born; therefore, with all His attributes, so the true reality of life has no room for the illusions of what someone wants it to be. Life truly is what we make of it. We need to allow ourselves to let loose what other people think and feel about us. Instead, in truth—*real* truth—we must honor ourselves. We need to be upright, responsible, and share our Father's wealth freely. We need to be aware; through our awareness, our strength builds. We must be patient with ourselves, trust what our Father tells us to do, and *do* it. Then, we accept life as it comes. Let's face it. How can our Father be wrong?

HOW DO WE ACCEPT WHO WE ARE?

We need to be patient and kind and affirm our self-worth. We refuse the appearance of circumstances, and instead relax into our Father's awareness. We ask for help and guidance in each moment and situation. We stop buying into the dullness and turmoil of the appearance of things. We dig deeper into ourselves for the answers. We do so based on humility and the true intention of wanting to know who we are. We allow judgment to give way to perception. We let perception give way to knowledge. We let knowledge give way to our Father's love. We refuse the coloring of the past and move freely in the present. We accept ourselves, with all our ugly warts, as well as our very special talents that are unique to us.

The past stays intact with preconceived notions, which translates into rigidity and stagnation. Through this viewpoint, we continually see the past. Life does not work that way. Instead, it moves, swirls, jumps, and turns upside down. With the right armor of realizing our self-worth as a descendent, a child of our Father, we experience its flow by resting in our own life preserver of self-assurance. We are proud of our heritage. We do not have to work for something our Father is willing to give us. We just have to be willing to accept it. We drop our shame and feelings of inadequacy. We affirm our true self-worth. We accept our Father's love.

HOW IS OUR INNER CONFLICT RESOLVED WITHIN OURSELVES AND WITH OTHERS?

We carry on in a continual battle within ourselves, which leaves us battered and weak. In its extreme, it leaves us tired, tense, and with little energy to see ourselves, even through uneventful days. We keep trying to keep everything together. We work hard to keep our lives from being upsetting; however, paradoxically, it causes us to be *more* upset, because life is not going the way we wanted it to. Life is just going to be life. Circumstances always change, as new events insert themselves into play. Being upset at a change in routine or expectations only causes internal disruption. Although, at times, we fare well in our day, we may still practice being upset when others are upset. We want everything to be smoothed out and without turmoil. Then, when we take on others' turmoil to avoid a conflict with them, we drive their condition into ourselves, thereby turning our mind and body into their falsified views and immature feelings.

We stand in conflict with ourselves, and yearn to break the cycle of servitude to a relentless world of insecurities and negative thinking that continues to drown in its own making. We must choose a viewpoint of positivity and light-heartedness, along with a sincere compassion not only for the other person but also for ourselves. If we are truly honest and caring about ourselves, we would refuse to let life's circumstances and other people's feelings, emotions, and manipulation wreak havoc upon our mind and body. As we admit this weakness, we now pray for strength that enlightens us to a fresh life, filled with more laughter, less heartache, and the promise of hope that only comes through the awareness and love of our Father, which sustains us and releases us from this treadmill of conflict.

HOW DO WE KNOW WE ARE NOT ALONE?

The world is not going to bend to our will. It will do its best to rake us over the coals and have us for dinner. It won't give to us, but instead it will look for opportunities to take from us and leave us with little or nothing. We must relax and accept it. That won't change. That is how the world works. It has no vision and no conscience. Based on all these dismal views, we don't have to fold up our tent and head for the desert. Life can still be enjoyable. We just have to be aware and flow with it. We just need to relax. It is not that bad. We are not destined to just creep along on our own. We listen for our Father's whisper, which makes us aware we are a gem, and we hold life in the palm of our hand.

Awareness comes from work. Although it is work, our Father gives us the tools to complete it. We are not out there with a pick and shovel. Our Father has turned over His steam shovel, along with a crew of angels to help us. We need to take our Father up on His offer of help. It just makes our life easier. All we need do is hop on that steam shovel and start her up. Yes, things do look dismal at times. Our frustrations rise, our anger surges, and we act foolishly. We say or do something ignorantly, which makes matters even worse. We just need to relax. Our Father gives us the tools to be successful in this game of life. We sit back, relax, and enjoy the ride. We even toot our horn once in a while. It could be fun. We just need to try it. We let life be. We have our Father on our side. What a wonderful ride!

HOW DO WE ACKNOWLEDGE OUR SUCCESSES?

It is easy enough to think it, and it is easy enough to say it. The fact of the matter is we need to believe it, and in the act of believing, we are doing it. The words, "be proud of yourself and your successes," do not mean anything unless we take them into our heart. We feel the words. We let our mind embrace them. We feel our body straightening up and watch our walk be more determined and confident. We go through our activities at the end of the day, and we are proud and happy with ourselves. We accept our failures as well. They are great teachers that lead us to our accomplishments.

Accepting our rewards builds confidence. This leads and carries us to more challenging endeavors that expand our soul and make us realize who we really are. What great gifts we possess! We use them proudly and with courage. We kneel at the altar of our Father and thank Him. We feel a sense of calmness and power. We stay focused on our mission and are flexible with the means to achieve our goals. Life unfolds as we let it. We let our Father take over our mind and heart. In that very act, confidence and strength are instilled in us and in those willing to listen to our words and recognize our actions. We pray daily for strength and guidance. We are always humble and yet confident, as life bows and opens its doors to us. By our acts of sharing, we are expanding the universe. We let our Father be born in us. We acknowledge who we are and our accomplishments.

HOW DO WE KNOW OUR FATHER IS WITH US?

Life is meant to be enjoyed, and enjoy it we must. It holds a wealth of happiness for us to explore and experience. As we relax, we claim the God-given power within ourselves and become more aware of who we really are. We stop striving and straining, and instead start enjoying the gifts our Father bestows on us. As we realize our relationship with our Father, we become calm, serene, and powerful, with focus and intent. Life slows down to a pleasant rhythm, and we flow with it. This calmness allows our good to flow to us so we can enjoy it. Our heart rests lighter and our mind clears, so we move with more ease. The present comes to meet us with each new and refreshing moment.

This good, we must realize and claim. This is our true heritage. Our charge is to be proud of ourselves and confident with our actions. We must stop wavering, but instead act with authority and connection to our True Self. As we pray today, we must then wait for our guidance. We are proud and confident. We give thanks for our life. We accept the world the way it is, and we change our perceptions based on our Father's guidance. We stand tall, proud, and confident, realizing we are our Father's child, whom he loves endearingly and absolutely,—without question. May we realize the same love for Him, as we vow to devote our life to His will.

WHERE DO WE FIND THE TRUTH?

We search incessantly in all the wrong places for answers. We ponder better times and circumstances, and wish for many things we do not have. Our wandering thoughts bring us no peace and give us no satisfactory answers. Instead, when we settle ourselves, relax, and let go of our yearnings, the awareness of the peace of our Father is awakened in us. The peace that comes fills us. It nurtures our heart and brings clarity to our mind. It puts us in the flow of life, and we become a passenger on our journey as our Father steers our course. Life is meant to be enjoyed with fervor and warmth. Every bit of strength we possess comes from our Father. All of our weaknesses come from our own yearnings for circumstances to be to *our* liking, so we will "feel safe." Our salvation lies in faith and our commitment to our heavenly Father. He looks at us endearingly and waits for us to come home to Him. Father, we ask you to give us strength to seek You only and love You only.

HOW DO WE ASK FOR HELP?

We continually battle with ourselves as we try *so* hard to make things right, and also set our expectations so high, we are sure to get disappointed. We choose wishful thinking over our Father, and then we turn around and ask Him for help. We try so hard, it pushes our blessings away from us. We want things, but we do not accept the blessings we have. We must appreciate those first, right? We ask our Father for help, and yet we run around, pushing hard to keep everything in order.

The only hope we have is to humble ourselves, look deeply into our heart, and face the truth that we are powerless without our Father. Only by this admittance can we be free of disappointments and heartache. We watch our life smoothing out, because we are handling the everyday situations so much better. However, when we fail, we still get upset. We know we will finally succeed in those situations. We are our Father's child. He loves us and wants us home with Him. Only by being honest and loving with ourselves will we know Him. Only by ceasing our upheaval of emotions will we be triumphant in life. We need strength, our Father's strength. Without it, we are lost and without hope. Dear and Holy Father, have mercy on us and teach us to be Your servant. Wash the dirt and grime away that cover our soul. Bring us clarity and freshness with each moment. Let us see with clarity those we encounter. Most of all, help us to truly honor Your love and realize we are truly your children.

HOW DO WE CHANGE OUR THOUGHTS?

It is really easy to make ourselves upset, worried, and a mess, especially if we have been working at it for a long time. It feels natural, but, of course, it is all made-up. It is just an illusion. We created this state of mind. Our Father did not. He sees us fresh, vibrant, and full of life. He sees a calm and confident spirit, with unlimited capabilities and an unending capacity to share His love freely and without condition. It's a matter of choice. It is a choice to undo the false thinking that locks us in turmoil, confusion, and a forlorn outlook that our state of mind will never change. So, as we ask for help from our Father, we release the tension. As we let go of the habit of worry thoughts, we enjoy ourselves. We see our productivity rise. We see our true personality. We see our own easiness and true nature. We live in the now, and enjoy our life more fully and with courage. Father, hear our prayer, clear our mind, and help us to allow ourselves to accept our life exactly the way it is, with all its numerous and profound blessings.

HOW DO WE STOP ILL THOUGHTS?

Thoughts can be an instrument to achieve peace or a constant reminder of what we think life should be like. As thoughts churn and we desire to have more and more of what we want, it brings on an unnatural cycle that leaves us in a wasteland of tiredness with no end in sight. It racks our mind and body with stress and leaves no room for relaxation and enjoyment. Sure, things get hectic. Sure, things are not the way we want them to be. Sure, someone cut us off on the freeway, or our spouse said something that upset us this morning. Still, thoughts are the bridge to our very own perceptions, and perceptions are the bridge to the knowledge of our Father Himself. We must relax and stop the churning, worry, and "what if's" that continually traverse our mind. Instead, we must consciously sit for a while, and bring our thoughts to a slow crawl. We stop the madness of the churning of our thoughts.

Once we have stopped them, we release them. Then, our Father presents Himself to us. At this point, we have chosen our Father, and not our own thoughts and desires. Does all of this take practice? Well, of course, but the reward is so great, it dwarfs the meaningless thoughts we tool around and spin like a hamster wheel in our mind. The only value lies in the mind's ability to know our Father. As the mind learns to free itself, the heart takes over. As the heart softens and becomes less rigid and open, it is able to unite with our Father. There, thoughts do not exist. Instead, feelings of unity and love do.

HOW DO WE VENTURE FORTH INTO OUR TRUE LIFE?

A nagging recurring theme in our mind keeps us trapped in the constraints of our own fears and insecurities. We think: be safe, *just* be safe. Yet the irony of it keeps us in tension and turmoil. The free-flowing nature of life is where security lies. There, our Father provides everlasting love, support, and sustenance for our mind and heart. Sorrow envelops a safe existence, and it darkens the light that shines from our soul.

Existence in a sorrowful state is simply that. We sleep, we wake, we haul into work, and then back again. We turn on the TV for a short while, and then do the same thing all over again. The true value of life lies in the exploration of our own consciousness and the discovery of our very own uniqueness, filled by our Father's all-powerful nature. The beauty of our uniqueness is displayed, as we choose to allow the light of our soul to shine through. We must let our Father sustain us. We take the "unsafe" journey, and discover a world and life that unfold uniquely, just for us. Of course, we must earn our way through life, and we must conquer the fears we think keep us "safe." Only in this way can we stay "forever young" and eternal.

HOW DO WE SEE PAST APPEARANCES?

It seldom turns out the way we expect, so the message is to stop expecting. Hard work *does* yield positive results. They just might not be the ones we were planning on. We need to stop thinking with our head, and instead "think" with our heart. We must follow our heart with true honesty and absolute certainty. The circumstances we see with our senses might very well deceive us, because perception is superficial. We must dig deeper into our soul for the real answers;

that is where the truth resides. We look at the content, not the form. The substance of life itself is the true reality. That substance is our Father Himself. All else is a manufactured existence. There is no room for wavering.

We need to trust our Father, our intuition, that small voice that whispers to us when we really listen. That is our true reality, and that is what sets us free. In that way, we are acting in accordance with our Father. He provides us the strength to break through the manufactured outlook we have created for ourselves. We rest in the knowledge that we are never abandoned and never forsaken. We listen intently with our whole heart to that soft whisper that comes from inside us. We look past the circumstances our eyes see and minds understand to be true. Instead, we enjoy the sight that comes from our heart. That and only that is real.

HOW DO WE DECIDE TO BE HAPPY?

What seems to be a mystery is that we do not enjoy ourselves. It is not a mystery, however—it is just a decision. In every moment, we possess the gift to choose life itself as it unfolds before us, or choose the past that haunts us with our made-up fears and insecurities. The answer is awareness; through awareness, perceptions change. As our perceptions change, we understand more, because we see ourselves and life more clearly.

As we perceive more clearly, we enjoy life more, because we feel less threatened and more inclined to follow our nature, which allows us to be happy. So, today, we decide to see our insecurities, acknowledge them, admit to them when we see them, and then let them go. What is left? That is the enjoyment of life. It's the sweet, sweet mystery of our Father Himself, as He unfolds Himself especially to us, with all His infinite love. We speak to Him today, and we pray He answers us. Our life literally depends on it.

WHY DO WE CHOOSE OUR FATHER ABOVE ALL ELSE?

The answer truly lies in our heart. We give ourselves peace. We release the manufactured thoughts from our mind that we created in the past. They hold no value for us and present a tumultuous view of the world. It does not make any sense to walk around with rose-colored glasses either. This also destroys our peace. We must be truly honest with ourselves, be aware of our innermost feelings, and listen intently to what they are telling us. If anxiety and fear are a constant presence, we must ask ourselves why. There is no need for those thoughts. They were born from our own mind years ago, and we have provided them safe harbor. We must look very deeply into our soul. There, our Father waits patiently for us and knows we will call Him. We must grant ourselves peace. We must eradicate any thoughts that are not His. We let Him teach us how to live. In that way, we love fully and unencumbered. We are a free spirit.

HOW DO WE STOP FALSE THINKING?

The flurry of thoughts that races in our mind hypes us up to an artificial rhythm that consumes most of our energy. This heightened state keeps us in a constant stressful condition. In this way, we have no reserve to use when conditions of our life escalate and cause further demands upon us. When life throws more our way, we strain to meet its demands and are at its mercy. Life tosses us around, like a bottle in the ocean. As we turn to our Father for help, He replies to us with understanding and compassion. He urges us to remember who we truly are. Through our mind, joined with His, we begin to realize our heritage and understand the workings of true life. Then, we know how to handle the world.

Through our Father's guidance, we find our way. Now, we are able to see our mind and change how it works. As we take control of our thoughts, our life flows into an easy rhythm. Our heart eases. Our body rests, and our breath deepens. Our digestive system soothes itself. We are perfectly at ease, confident, and fully aware. Our journey has taken us to this point. Now, we must learn to control our thoughts, so our life manifests according to our Father's laws. We vow now to practice to slow down unproductive thoughts, stop them, and then drop them from our mind. In this way, we walk free and unencumbered, as children of our Father. We are a natural child of God. This is our heritage.

CONCLUSION

Your steadfastness to the words in this book has been proven by your shift in consciousness. The answers that you have been seeking have been revealed to you as you have allowed them to come. Your true devotion on this never-ending journey you have embarked upon proves sacred as you awaken to your True Self. Your intent must be one pointed and focused as you take each step toward self aware- ness. As you awaken, you find that you can never go back; and in that truth you find strength and joy. Your choice has brought you to this point and your choice will carry you forward on the road before you. Your awakening gives rise to self remembering – and isn't that what you have been seeking?

There is nothing more important than finding the truth. Be assured that you are making the right steps toward that goal. Let the insights you have gained from this book bring you the inspiration to lead your life the way you were meant to. Allow your thoughts to be turned from old worn out ideas that no longer serve you to new refreshing thinking that no longer restricts and binds you, but lifts you up to the true and powerful being you really are. Take heart as the road gets tougher and the obstacles loom larger before you, knowing that the strength you are building is the strength you need in order to know the truth that lives within you. Good travels, on your road to freedom and fulfillment.

Finally, I leave you with a poem I wrote many years ago.

Inside Your Soul

From open hearts and minds lie the secrets of our souls.
From a smile and caring is happiness discovered.
From vision and clarity is a world seen in need.
From friendship and time spent is sharing and enrichment.
From the earth to heaven's gate is our journey made.
From opportunity is confidence born.
From each moment realizations come.
Stay in the now and be with it for there are your gifts.

APPENDIX 1: WHAT IS CHANNELED WRITING?

I shared a brief description of Channeled Writing in the Introduction of this book, but want to expand a bit further, not only to describe my own process but to share that you too channel in your own way: we all do.

As I mentioned earlier, channeled writing is not exotic for me nor does it occur in an altered or trance state. Instead, the words come in moments of quiet when I allow them to come without thinking. Sometimes, the words cannot wait to get on the page. At other times, different words seem to filter down like you would see a feather or a leaf falling to the ground. In this case, when it feels right, the words then start to come out on the page.

How and why did this channeled writing start for me.? The only thing I can figure is the spiritual work I had done cleared the way for it to come through. I am eternally thankful and very, very humbled by this gift. I feel very fortunate to share these words with you.

I find it similar to turning on a particular channel on a car radio. There is a certain frequency that the radio is being tuned into. The music simply comes on unobstructed. If the signal is weak or there is static, the music is not heard clearly or it goes in and out. The weak signal occurs for me when I am really, really tired so the words just do not come. The static comes when my own thoughts are in the way and the words cannot come through clearly

I am a writer so it only makes sense that I would do channeled writing. However, we all have channeled in some way whether we were aware of it or not. You may have heard of a musician, while at the airport waiting for a flight, who wrote a hit song in 20 or 30 minutes. Music is their talent and the song just came to them. Another example would be an athlete. Take a baseball player in the outfield who is running full out to catch a fly ball, at times with their back to the ball. How did they make that catch?! I do not know but what I do know is they are channeling, not thinking, but simply expressing their athletic prowess. Lastly, we can see the natural energy and exuberance of small children. Have you ever walked by a school when the children are out on recess and heard their laughter and saw their energy being freely expressed? Are they thinking about what they are going to do next or are they just expressing themselves by playing with abandonment. It is free flowing expression unencumbered by personal thoughts. This is channelling to me.

Channeling, in my case channeled writing, may seem mysterious, however, as I mentioned earlier it is simply natural. It seems mysterious because we are so removed from it by the thoughts we've built up around ourselves for so many years. We do not really express ourselves anymore. Everyone has unique talents and abilities that need to be expressed but instead they have put them aside in exchange for doing other things the way everyone else does them, e.g. career, family, mortgage, and so on. It is easy for us to fall into conventional thinking. However, we are all quite different and unique. I bet for some of you there is a musical instrument, for example, a guitar stuck in the back of a closet or down in the basement that has not been touched for a number of years. Maybe the same thing is true for others who have paint brushes that have not touched a canvas in many years. Again, we all channel who we really are. Since we forgot how; it may seem mysterious.

In closing, I could have gone out to the Internet and Googled channeled writing, pieced parts of the different sources together, and I believe I could have come up with a good description. However, I decided to channel the above words to you. I feel that you deserve that. We are all souls upon this earth together and we need to respect and honor each others' self expression. So I say to you, keep channeling away. I want to see the fruits of who you really are as you freely express yourselves.

For those of you who want to find out more about channeled writing, please refer to the Resources section at the end of this book.

APPENDIX 2: TRUE FRIENDS

(To Francine)

But by God's grace we met and slowly built the ties of friendship. To reach across to another soul and share secrets that few, if any, have known, evokes a trust which sets us free. Rarely does this occurrence display itself. Graciously I accept this gift and walk hand in hand with my friend. Daily our talks provide a refuge for me from a hectic day and for you from the tedium of narrow minds with complaints as their single purpose. The words flow freely and understanding comes with no explanations. Wisdom sits in that room and the touch of God's love lets us share special moments. For as one gives to the other, each receives in kind; and for a short time, we step into eternity. God sees us and grins as His two children share His love.

RESOURCES

Writing the Divine: How to Use Channeling for Soul Growth & Healing by Sara Wiseman. (Llewellyn Publications, 2009)

This book should answer most if not all of your questions about channeled writing.

The Impersonal Life by Joseph Benner (DeVorss Publications, 1949)

After I found this book in the bookstore, I read it three times in a row I was so taken with it. It is my favorite spiritual book. It is channeled writing.

How You Can Talk With God by Paramahansa Yogananda (Self-Realization Fellowship, 1957)

I like having this by my side table in my office so I can pick it up at any time.

A New Earth: Awakening to Your Life's Purpose by Eckhart Tolle (Penguin, 2008)

Eckhart Tolle is my favorite modern day spiritual author. Although he is noted for his book *The Power of Now*, I am partial to *A New Earth*. Oprah had a ten-part podcast series with Eckhart Tolle a number of years ago which I really enjoyed.

ABOUT THE AUTHOR

With five decades of deeply devoted spiritual practice and exploration, Patrick Schiavone's spiritual journey has culminated in these writings of the *From Quiet Moments* trilogy. This fulfills his life's purpose of providing others the wisdom needed to travel their own spiritual path with more ease and comfort. He is currently enjoying retirement with his wife of more than 40 years. They now have the time for long conversations or to simply observe nature.